NATIONAL COUNCIL OF WELFARE REPORTS

WELFARE INCOMES 2002

SPRING 2003

Copies of this publication may be obtained from

National Council of Welfare
9th Floor, 112 Kent Street
Ottawa, Ontario K1A 0J9
(613) 957-2961
Fax: (613) 957-0680
E-mail: ncw@magi.com
Web Site: www.ncwcnbes.net

Également disponible en français sous le titre:
Revenus de bien-être social 2002

Cat. No. H68-27/2002E
ISBN 0-662-33817-0

Canadian Publications Mail # 40065597

TABLE OF CONTENTS

115726

ACKNOWLEDGMENTS

The National Council of Welfare is grateful to the officials of the provincial and territorial governments who took the time to review the factual material in this report and previous reports.

The Council also appreciates the continuing support and cooperation of the Quantitative and Information Analysis Division of the Social Policy Directorate at Human Resources Development Canada, in particular the help of Anne Tweddle and Carole Broome.

The Council would also like to thank the staff at Statistics Canada for providing the most recent statistics on low income cut-offs and average incomes in Canada that are referenced in this report.

FOREWORD

Welfare Incomes is a regular report on the welfare rates in each province and territory in Canada. This report estimates welfare incomes for four types of households in 2002: a single employable person, a single person with a disability, a single-parent family with a two-year-old child, and a two-parent family with two children aged ten and 15. The National Council of Welfare has published similar estimates since 1986.

Welfare Incomes has never been a good-news report, and this issue is, unfortunately, no change. The gap between the poverty line and welfare incomes remained large and relatively unchanged in 2002 with people on welfare subsisting on as little as one-fifth of the poverty line. People on welfare continued to realize an even smaller fraction of the average income of other Canadians. Most welfare incomes have failed to keep pace with inflation, leaving the welfare poor poorer than ever.

When the Council looked at provincial and territorial contributions to welfare incomes for families with children, we found they had eroded badly. For families on welfare, the provinces and territories contributed a decreasing share every year even as the federal government made increasingly larger contributions through the National Child Benefit. Provincial and territorial governments realized savings on welfare – and all at the cost of the poorest of parents and children.

This is a disappointing situation, particularly more than four years after the federal government made a massive infusion of cash to low-income families with children through the National Child Benefit. While the federal government gave a basic child tax benefit and an additional supplement to all low-income parents, most provincial and territorial governments chose to claw back the supplement from those parents unlucky enough to depend on welfare. Only Newfoundland and New Brunswick resisted the temptation from the outset. More recently, Nova Scotia, Quebec, and Manitoba decided to limit their clawback of the supplement to the federal child benefit. But the amount of money provincial and territorial governments gave to the poorest of parents and children still declined in most jurisdictions. The Council was particularly disappointed to note that this occurred as overwhelming evidence emerged that underlined the importance of early child development.

In the focus on child poverty, it is easy to lose sight of the conditions facing others on welfare. This year's report shows the desperate situation facing those people the welfare system considers employable. After years of cuts and freezes to their welfare incomes, this group was forced to subsist on incomes as low as one-fifth of the poverty line in 2002. Similarly, the report tracks the slow decline in the value of the welfare incomes of people with disabilities. This group was generally spared the major cuts to their benefits that faced those considered employable, but their incomes declined slowly as inflation took its toll.

The National Council of Welfare continues to be concerned about the levels of poverty of anyone who is unfortunate enough to be forced to rely on welfare. Children live in families and in communities, and those children raised in poverty eventually grow up. There is no age or stage of life at which the Council believes anyone should be expected to live at the level of abject poverty the Canadian welfare system provides.

I. WHAT IS WELFARE?

Social assistance or welfare is the income program of last resort in Canada. It provides money to individuals and families whose resources are inadequate to meet their needs and who have exhausted other avenues of support.

Until March 31, 1996, welfare was paid under the terms of the Canada Assistance Plan (CAP), an arrangement that allowed the cost to be shared by the federal government and the provinces and territories. On April 1, 1996, the Canada Health and Social Transfer (CHST) replaced CAP. Under the CHST, the federal government reduced its transfer payments to the provinces and territories for health, education and social services. As of July 1, 1998, the National Child Benefit which consists of the basic Canada Child Tax Benefit (CCTB) and the National Child Benefit Supplement (NCBS) has covered some of the cost of welfare for families with children.

Although people talk about welfare as a single entity, there are really 13 welfare systems in Canada: one in each province and territory. Despite the fact that each of the 13 systems is different, they have many common features. They have complex rules which regulate all aspects of the system, including eligibility for assistance, the rates of assistance, the amounts of other income recipients are allowed to keep, and the way in which applicants and recipients may question decisions regarding their cases.

ELIGIBILITY

Eligibility for welfare is based on general administrative rules that vary widely throughout the country. For example, applicants must be of a certain age, usually between 18 and 65. Full-time students of post-secondary educational institutions qualify for assistance in some provinces and territories only if they meet stringent conditions. In other provinces and territories, students cannot apply for assistance without leaving their studies. Parents must try to secure any court-ordered maintenance support to which they are entitled. People with a disability require medical certification of their conditions. Strikers are not eligible in most jurisdictions. Immigrants must try to obtain financial assistance from their sponsors.

Once applicants meet the administrative conditions, they go through a "needs test." The welfare department compares the budgetary needs of an applicant and any dependants with the assets and income of the household. Needs, assets and income are defined in provincial and territorial welfare laws. In general, welfare is granted when a household's non-exempted financial resources are less than the cost of regularly recurring needs that the welfare department considers acceptable, for example, food, shelter, household, personal and special needs.

First, the needs test examines applicants' fixed and liquid assets. In most provinces and territories, fixed assets such as a principal residence, furniture and clothing are considered exempt. Most provinces and territories also exempt the value of a car, although some jurisdictions take into consideration factors such as the need for a private vehicle and the availability of public transportation. Property and equipment required for employment are generally considered exempt. Applicants are usually required to convert any non-exempt fixed assets into liquid assets and to use any non-exempt liquid assets for their ongoing needs before qualifying for welfare.

The limits on liquid assets (that is, cash, bonds and securities that are readily convertible to cash) appear in Table 1.1. The amounts vary by household size and employability. Where a household's liquid assets are higher than the amounts in Table 1.1, that household is not entitled to welfare until the excess is spent on approved needs. The amounts shown in Table 1.1 are the liquid asset exemption levels that were in effect in January 2002.

After welfare departments examine the fixed and liquid assets of welfare applicants, they identify all the sources of income for that household. Welfare departments generally consider that income from other sources such as employment, pensions and Employment Insurance is fully available for support of the household. Some types of income, such as the basic federal child tax benefit (but not the supplement) and the federal GST credit, are normally considered exempt in the determination of eligibility for welfare.

Finally, welfare departments subtract all non-exempt income from the total needs of the household. Applicants qualify for welfare if their household's needs are greater than the household's resources or if there is a budget surplus that is insufficient to meet the cost of a special need such as medications or disability-related equipment.

The needs test was the central eligibility criterion required by the assistance provisions of the Canada Assistance Plan. The law authorized the federal government to share with the provinces and territories the costs of welfare only on behalf of households that qualified on the basis of need. Since the Canada Health and Social Transfer replaced the Canada Assistance Plan in April 1996, provinces and territories are no longer required to use a needs test to qualify for federal contributions to their welfare programs. As of the date of this report, however, no province or territory has replaced its needs test.

TABLE 1.1: LIQUID ASSET EXEMPTION LEVELS AS OF JANUARY 2002

	Unemployable			Employable	
	Single Person	Single Parent, One Child	Single Person with Disability	Single Person	Family
NEWFOUNDLAND AND LABRADOR	$500	$1,500	$3,000[1]	$500	$1,500
PRINCE EDWARD ISLAND	N/A[2]	$1,200	$900	$50 to $200[3]	$1,800[4]
NOVA SCOTIA[5]	$500	$1,000	$500	Province generally requires applicants to exhaust liquid assets to meet basic needs.	
NEW BRUNSWICK	$1,000	$2,000	$3,000	$1,000	$2,000
QUEBEC[6]	$2,500	$2,825[7]	$2,500	$1,500	$2,917[8]
ONTARIO[9]	$0[10]	$5,500	$5,000	$520	Adult, one child: $1,457 Couple: $901 Couple, one child: $1,530 Each additional dependant child: $500

TABLE 1.1: LIQUID ASSET EXEMPTION LEVELS AS OF JANUARY 2002

	Unemployable			Employable	
	Single Person	Single Parent, One Child	Single Person with Disability	Single Person	Family
MANITOBA	N/A[11]	$2,000	$2,000	$0 at enrolment $400 after enrollment[12]	$0 at enrolment $1,600 after enrolment
SASKATCHEWAN	$1,500	$3,000	$1,500	$1,500	Adult, one child: $3,000 Each additional dependant child: $500
ALBERTA	$1,500	$2,500	$1,500[13]	$50 cash plus the equivalent of $1,450 in cash assets	$250 cash plus the equivalent of $2,250 in cash assets
BRITISH COLUMBIA[14]	$1,500[15]	$2,500[16]	$3,000	$1,500[17]	$2,500[18]
YUKON[19]	$500	$1,500	$1,500	$500	Couple, two children: $1,600
NORTHWEST TERRITORIES	The director may determine that some assets should not be converted into cash for social or economic reasons and that they are therefore not considered as a personal resource.				

NATIONAL COUNCIL OF WELFARE

TABLE 1.1: LIQUID ASSET EXEMPTION LEVELS AS OF JANUARY 2002

	Unemployable			Employable	
	Single Person	Single Parent, One Child	Single Person with Disability	Single Person	Family
NUNAVUT	The director may determine that some assets (such as those used in traditional activities) should not be converted into cash for social or economic reasons and that they are therefore not considered as a personal resource.				

Newfoundland and Labrador

[1] To qualify for a liquid asset exemption of $3,000 for a single disabled person, the disabled person must require supportive services to aid independent living.

Prince Edward Island

[2] Single applicants were not considered unemployable unless they were disabled.

[3] For unemployable applicants who required welfare for less than four months, the exemption was $50. For a single person on welfare for four months or more, the liquid asset exemption level was $200.

[4] For persons with dependants who were on welfare for four months or more, liquid asset exemption levels were $1,200 per couple and $300 for each child for a total of $1,800.

Nova Scotia

[5] In 2001, liquid asset exemption levels were decreased from $2,500 to $1,000 for an unemployable single parent and from $3,000 to $500 for an unemployable single person with disability.

Quebec

[6] In 1998, Quebec set standard maximum liquid asset amounts according to family size. If the applicant's assets (including expected income from other sources during the month of application) fell below the maximum, the welfare cheque for that month was calculated based on the rest of the days left in that month. Heating and utilities costs were deducted from total assets. Amounts increased in January 2001.

[7] The exemption level for the single parent was $2,500 plus $325 for one child for a total of $2,825. If the single parent with one child had severe limitations to work, the level was $5,000 plus $325 for the child for a total of $5,325.

[8] The exemption level for an employable couple was $2,500 plus $417 for two children, which totals $2,917. The exemption level for an employable couple with only one child was $2,500 plus $217 for a total of $2,717.

Ontario

[9] The "unemployable" category was the Ontario Disability Support Program; the "employable" category was Ontario Works. The Ontario Disability Support Program allowed assets beyond the prescribed limit provided the funds were intended for the purchase of an approved disability-related item or service or an item or service necessary for the health of a member of the welfare recipient's family. The asset exemption level for a couple under the Ontario Disability Support Program was $7,500.

[10] The liquid asset exemption for an unemployable single person was $5,000 in 2001 but was eliminated for 2002.

Manitoba

[11] Single applicants were not considered unemployable unless they were disabled.

[12] At the time of enrollment, there was no liquid asset exemption for employable singles and couples. After enrollment, liquid asset exemptions were $400 for a single person and $1,600 for a couple with two children.

Alberta

[13] This rate refers to people who received welfare under the Supports for Independence program. Alberta granted an exemption of up to $3,000 if a person was severely and permanently disabled and had high needs because of the costs of personal support services. Most people with severe disabilities received benefits under the Assured Income for the Severely Handicapped (AISH) program.

British Columbia

[14] Effective April 2002, in the first month of welfare the liquid asset exemption was the welfare rate plus an additional $150 for singles (a total of $860); the social assistance rate plus $250 for families with dependents (a total of $1,096 for single parent and $1,241 for the couple with two children); and $3,000 total for the disabled. These rates will be reflected in future editions of this report.

[15] The liquid asset exemption for an unemployable single person was increased from $500 to $1,500 as of January 2002 for recipients who were on welfare in the previous month. Otherwise, the asset exemption was the welfare rate only for the first month.

[16] The liquid asset exemption for an unemployable single parent with one child decreased from $5,000 to $2,500 as of January 2002 for recipients who were on welfare in the previous month. Otherwise, the asset exemption was the welfare rate only for the first month.

[17] The liquid asset exemption for an employable single person was increased from $500 to $1,500 as of January 2002 for recipients who were on welfare in the previous month. Otherwise, the asset exemption was the welfare rate only for the first month.

[18] The liquid asset exemption for an employable couple decreased from $5,500 plus $500 for each child to $2,500 total as of January 2002 for recipients who were on welfare in the previous month. Otherwise, the asset exemption was the welfare rate only for the first month.

Yukon

[19] The exemption level for employables applies to people on assistance for less than 90 days. Higher levels are permitted for those on assistance for more than 90 days.

RATES OF ASSISTANCE

Every province and territory uses a different method of calculating basic welfare which generally includes food, clothing, shelter, utilities, and an allowance for personal and household needs.

Applicants and recipients may be eligible for extra assistance in most provinces and territories if they have special needs such as medication, prosthetic devices, technical aids and equipment, special clothing or dental care. Welfare departments provide cash or "in kind" support in the form of vouchers, goods or services.

Sometimes applicants require assistance only for a special-needs item such as medication but they are able to provide for other basic needs from their own resources. In such cases, a province or territory may grant the specific amount that the household requires, provided that the applicants are eligible under the needs test.

Every province and territory has a list of special needs for which it will provide extra assistance. In some cases, only a portion of the cost of a particular item is paid. For example, the province or territory may reimburse a certain percentage of dental costs, and the recipient is expected to pay the remaining amount.

Across Canada, welfare officials have some degree of discretion in deciding whether certain households qualify for special assistance under provincial or territorial welfare regulations. Discretion is both a strength and weakness of the welfare system. On one hand, welfare recognizes the fact that individuals may have ongoing or one-time special needs for which they require assistance. On the other hand, a person with special needs may be considered eligible for extra assistance by one welfare worker, but not by another.

Table 1.2 presents a national picture of estimated welfare incomes for 2002. The incomes shown are for the basic needs of four household types: a single employable person, a single person with a disability, a single-parent family with a two-year-old child, and a two-parent family with two children aged ten and 15. When we calculated the welfare incomes, we assumed that each of the households went on welfare on January 1, 2002, and remained on welfare for the entire calendar year.

The figures in the table must be interpreted with caution. They are estimates. Welfare is a highly individualized program of income support, so every applicant could be eligible for a different amount of financial assistance because of the circumstances in his or her household. In addition, our calculations only consider cash income, since it is impossible for us to take into account the value of the services provided by a province or territory.

It is especially important to understand the derivation of the social assistance figures in Column 1. These figures are both maximum and minimum amounts. They are maximum amounts in that they represent the highest level of welfare that a designated province or territory will provide to a given household unit for its basic living needs. These rates can be reduced for a number of reasons. For example, legislation in all jurisdictions allows welfare authorities to reduce, cancel or suspend benefits if an employable recipient refuses a reasonable job offer, or quits a job without just cause. These figures are also <u>minimum</u> amounts in that they do not generally include special-needs assistance to which a given household may be entitled, such as costs related to a disability or the cost of searching for a job.

BASIC SOCIAL ASSISTANCE

The column called Basic Social Assistance in Table 1.2 shows the basic welfare that eligible households are entitled to have. Basic assistance generally includes an amount for food, clothing, shelter, utilities, personal and household needs. The figures in the basic social assistance column also reflect the reduction in assistance caused by the clawback of the National Child Benefit Supplement (NCBS) that began in July 1998 in the jurisdictions that clawed back.

To ensure to the greatest extent possible the comparability of the data, we made a number of assumptions in calculating basic assistance. These assumptions concerning recipient households include where people lived, the ages of the children, the employability of the household head, the type of housing and the case history.

A. RESIDENCE

The welfare rates shown for each province or territory are for the largest municipal area. This is because maximum shelter allowances vary by region in many jurisdictions. Households living in smaller municipalities often receive lower benefits because their shelter costs are lower than in large urban centres (and most shelter allowances are based on actual shelter costs). Some provinces and territories offer supplements to compensate welfare households living in remote areas for higher living costs.

B. AGES OF CHILDREN

Welfare rates for families with children in this report are based on the assumption that the child in the one-parent family is two years old and the children in the two-parent family are ten and 15 years old. Some provinces and territories vary a family's entitlement with the age of each child in the household.

C. EMPLOYABILITY OF THE HOUSEHOLD HEAD

In Table 1.2, we assigned short-term rates of assistance (which are generally lower than long-term rates) to single employable individuals and couples with children in all jurisdictions. The rates for single parents are based on the employability classifications in each province and territory.

In all jurisdictions, we have based our calculations on the assumption that the person with a disability received welfare, not payments for special, long-term disability programs.

D. TYPE OF HOUSING

We assumed that the welfare households in this report are tenants in the private rental market rather than homeowners or social housing tenants. We also assumed that they did not share their accommodation. All provinces and the three territories reduce welfare entitlements when recipient households live in subsidized housing or share their housing.

Where shelter allowances do not include the cost of utilities, we added the cost of utilities to the shelter rates. We used maximum shelter rates in all jurisdictions.

E. CASE HISTORY

In order to "annualize" the rates for this report, we assumed that these four typical households started receiving welfare on January 1, 2002 and remained on assistance until the last day of the calendar year.

We calculated basic social assistance month by month for each category of recipient in each province and territory, taking into account increases or decreases in rates as of their effective dates within each year. We also assumed that welfare households did not have any income from paid work during the time they were on assistance.

F. SPECIAL ASSISTANCE

Welfare departments provide two kinds of assistance for special needs. Some supplementary allowances are paid automatically to recipients in certain groups, such as people with disabilities or parents with school-age children. These are the amounts that appear in the second column in Table 1.2. Examples of this type of special assistance include extra assistance for people with disabilities, money for school expenses, winter clothing allowances and Christmas allowances.

Welfare departments also provide a second kind of assistance for one-time special needs, including items such as funeral expenses, moving costs or emergency home repairs. We have not included this type of special assistance in this report because the special needs are established on a case-by-case basis by individual welfare workers. In some cases, approval is required from an administrator, director or designated professional such as a doctor.

We have incorporated special assistance in the second column of Table 1.2 only when welfare departments would automatically provide it to certain recipients. If the welfare recipient has to provide special reasons to qualify for this assistance, our figures exclude it.

FEDERAL CHILD TAX BENEFIT

The federal child tax benefit is now called the National Child Benefit. It consists of the basic Canada Child Tax Benefit (CCTB) and the National Child Benefit Supplement (NCBS). In Table 1.2, the Federal Child Tax Benefit column shows the basic benefit and the supplement, including increases on July 1, 2002.

The federal government paid a basic federal child tax benefit of $1,117 from July 2001 to June 2002 and $1,151 from July 2002 to December 2002 for each child under age 18 in most parts of Canada if the family income was under $32,000 and $32,960 respectively for these two periods. In all provinces and territories, there was an additional annual benefit of $221 for each child under age seven from July 2001 to June 2002 and $228 from July 2002 to December 2002. The basic federal child tax benefit is totally phased out once the net income of a family with two children or less exceeds $75,000.

From July 1998 to June 2000, the federal government provided all families with incomes under $20,921 with a supplement to the basic federal child tax benefit. This income threshold rose to $21,214 in July 2000 and to $21,744 in July 2001. In July 2002, the maximum income with which a family could qualify for the supplement was raised to $22,397.

The supplement was $1,255 from July 2001 to June 2002 then was raised to $1,293 from July 2002 to December 2002 if a family had one child. If a family had a second child, an additional supplement was paid at $1,055 from July 2001 to June 2002 then raised to $1,087 from July 2002 to December 2002.

A family with one child two years of age received the basic federal child tax benefit of $1,117. The family also received $221 for a child under seven and the federal supplement of $1,255 for the first child for the period July 2001 to June 2002. From July 2002 to December 2002, the family received $1,151 in the basic benefit, $228 for the child under seven, and the supplement of $1,293.

A couple with two children aged ten and fifteen received the basic federal child tax benefit of $1,117 for each child, and the combined supplements of $1,255 and $1,055 from July 2001 to June 2002. From July 2002 to December 2002, the two-parent family received the basic benefit of $1,151 for each child and the combined supplements of $1,293 and $1,087.

The provincial and territorial clawbacks to the federal child tax benefits are captured as reductions in the Basic Social Assistance column or in the Provincial/Territorial Child Benefits column.

PROVINCIAL AND TERRITORIAL CHILD BENEFITS

The Newfoundland and Labrador Child and Family Benefit was fully integrated with the federal child tax benefit which means it was delivered directly to families by the Canada Customs and Revenue Agency. It was $17 per month for one child and $43 per month for two children.

In Prince Edward Island, the basic welfare rate included a Healthy Child Allowance of $41 per month per child.

The Nova Scotia Child Benefit was fully integrated with the federal child tax benefit. It was $445 per year for one child and $645 per year for the second child for a total of $1,090 per year for a family with two children.

The New Brunswick Child Tax Benefit was $20.83 per month per child.

In Quebec, the provincial Family Allowance provided $108 per month for a single-parent family and $52.08 per month for each child.

In Ontario, there were no provincial child tax benefits.

In Manitoba, the provincial welfare benefit included a payment for a child in a single-parent family of $10.80 per month and an additional payment for a child aged six and under of $12 per month.

The Saskatchewan Child Tax Benefit was $20.83 for the first six months of 2002 and was reduced to $17.67 for the last six months for the first child in a family. The second child in a family received $37.83 and $35.17 per month for the same time period.

In Alberta, there were no provincial child tax benefits.

In British Columbia, the BC Family Bonus was $114.83 a child for the first six months and $116.42 a child for the last six months of 2002. BC then deducted the full amount of the National Child Benefit Supplement.

The Yukon Child Benefit provided a maximum of $300 per year for each child. The NWT Child Benefit was $330 per year and the Nunavut Child Benefit was $330 per year.

THE CLAWBACK OF THE NATIONAL CHILD BENEFIT SUPPLEMENT

The federal government provided the same basic federal child tax benefit to eligible families in all provinces and territories. The one exception was Alberta which asked the federal government to adjust the benefit depending upon the age of the child. But the supplement to the basic federal child tax benefit was treated differently from one province or territory to another. Some jurisdictions treated the supplement as unearned income and deducted it from basic welfare payments. Other jurisdictions reduced the overall rates for basic social assistance, provincial child benefits or the provincial family allowance to a lower level. The process varied, but the result was the same: these jurisdictions clawed back what represents a significant amount of income from families on welfare.

New Brunswick and Newfoundland did not reduce basic social assistance when the supplement was introduced and have allowed families to benefit fully from the basic federal child tax benefit and the supplement. All other provinces and territories reduced their basic social assistance or child and family benefits every year for the first few years after the supplement was introduced.

A few provinces have since allowed at least some families on welfare to retain a portion of the supplement. But even then, these provinces allow families to keep only the money from more recent supplements. The overall welfare incomes for these families were already reduced because of the clawbacks in the past. These families did not benefit from the original value of the supplement.

Prince Edward Island treated the supplement as non-exempt income and subtracted the amount from basic social assistance.

Prior to August 2001, Nova Scotia treated the supplement as non-exempt income and subtracted it from basic social assistance. In August 2001, the province eliminated personal allowances for all children under 18 while deciding to allow welfare recipients to keep the full provincial and federal child tax benefits. The total amount of the provincial child tax benefit and the federal child tax benefit and supplement was not as large as the personal allowances were. As a result, the couple with two children lost income while the province touted its cessation of the clawback.

Prior to July 2001, Quebec reduced the family allowance by the full value of the supplement. As of July 2001, Quebec no longer deducted annual increases to the supplement from the family allowance. The family allowance is now held at the July 2000 rate of $52.08 a month.

Ontario treated the supplement as non-exempt income and reduced basic social assistance by the full amount of the supplement each year.

Prior to July 2000, Manitoba treated the supplement as non-exempt income and subtracted it from basic social assistance for all families with children. From July 2000 to August 2001, a provincial supplement of $20 a month was added to the welfare payments of families with children under seven to compensate for the clawback of the federal supplement. Since July 2001, families with children under seven are allowed to keep the annual increase to the federal supplement. The federal supplement is still deducted from basic social assistance for families with children aged seven and over but at the rate set in July 1999.

The Saskatchewan Child Tax Benefit was reduced by the full value of the supplement and its increases each year. This provincial child tax benefit will eventually be eliminated if increases to the supplement continue to be deducted.

In Alberta, the basic federal child tax benefit was adjusted depending on the age of the child. For children under seven years of age, the basic benefit was reduced to $85.42 a month for the first six months of 2002 and then $87.92 for the last six months instead of the basic federal benefit of $93.08 and $95.92 a month for the same time periods in the rest of Canada. The ten-year-old child received $91.25 per month and the fifteen-year-old child received $102.08 per month for the first six months of 2002 and then $93.83 and $105 per month for the last six months of 2002. The federal supplement was then deducted dollar for dollar from basic social assistance.

In British Columbia, the BC Family Bonus was $114.83 a child each month for the first six months of 2002 and then $116.42 for the last six months. But the federal supplement was then fully deducted from these amounts for all low income families that were eligible for it – not just those families on welfare.

In the Yukon, Northwest Territories and Nunavut, the supplement was treated as non-exempt income and deducted dollar for dollar from basic social assistance.

As a result of the clawback, the already complex system of welfare programs has become even more complicated. With all the new rules and variations in welfare across the country, it is now almost impossible for welfare recipients to be sure that they are receiving all the benefits to which they are entitled.

The National Council of Welfare is very concerned by the fact that the clawbacks to the federal child tax benefit discriminate against families on welfare. Our 2001 report, *Child Poverty Profile 1998*, estimated that only 66 percent of poor families with children benefited from the federal child tax benefit between June 1998 and June 1999. Seventy-nine percent of poor two-parent families received the supplement, but only 57 percent of poor single-parent families were allowed to keep the supplement. As women head most single-parent families, we believe that this constitutes discrimination on the basis of gender.

GST CREDIT

The column for Federal GST Credit shows the federal refundable credit for the Goods and Services Tax or the federal portion of the Harmonized Sales Tax in the Atlantic provinces. The GST credit is paid quarterly if the family income was under $26,941 based upon 2000 tax year income and $27,749 based upon 2001 tax year income.

GST payments were received in January and April based upon 2000 tax year information and in July and October based upon 2001 tax year information. The four payments received in 2002 were worth a maximum of two payments at $51.75 each and two payments at $53.25 each per adult or the first child in a single-parent family for a total of $210.00. For other dependent children, the maximum was two payments at $27.25 each and two payments at $28.00 each for a total of $110.50.

Single adults also received an income-tested supplement in 2002 to a maximum of two payments at $27.25 each and two payments at $28.00 each for a total of $110.50 if their annual income was higher than $6,710 in 2000 or $6,911 in 2001.

PROVINCIAL TAX CREDITS

The tax credits in Column 6 are the provincial government refund of the Harmonized Sales Tax in Newfoundland and Labrador, the Sales and Property Tax Credits in Ontario and the Sales Tax Credit in British Columbia.

TABLE 1.2: ESTIMATED 2002 ANNUAL WELFARE INCOME BY TYPE OF HOUSEHOLD

	Basic Social Assistance	Additional Benefits	Federal Child Tax Benefit[1]	Provincial/ Territorial Child Benefits	Federal GST Credit[2]	Provincial/ Territorial Tax Credits	Total Income
NEWFOUNDLAND AND LABRADOR[3]							
Single Employable	$3,048				$210	$40	$3,298
Person with a Disability	$7,140	$1,500			$245	$40	$8,925
Single Parent, One Child	$11,436		$2,633	$204	$531	$100	$14,903
Couple, Two Children	$11,916		$4,613	$516	$641	$200	$17,886
PRINCE EDWARD ISLAND[4]							
Single Employable	$5,757				$210		$5,967
Person with a Disability[5]	$7,602	$1,110			$244		$8,956
Single Parent, One Child[6]	$9,814		$2,633		$531		$12,977
Couple, Two Children[7]	$14,473	$350	$4,613		$641		$20,077
NOVA SCOTIA[8]							
Single Employable	$4,980				$210		$5,190
Person with a Disability[9]	$8,580				$240		$8,820
Single Parent, One Child[10]	$8,760		$2,633	$445	$531		$12,368
Couple, Two Children[11]	$11,520		$4,613	$1090	$641		$17,864

TABLE 1.2: ESTIMATED 2002 ANNUAL WELFARE INCOME BY TYPE OF HOUSEHOLD

	Basic Social Assistance	Additional Benefits	Federal Child Tax Benefit[1]	Provincial/ Territorial Child Benefits	Federal GST Credit[2]	Provincial/ Territorial Tax Credits	Total Income
NEW BRUNSWICK							
Single Employable	$3,168				$210		$3,378
Person with a Disability	$6,696				$210		$6,906
Single Parent, One Child	$8,772	$900	$2,633	$250	$531		$13,085
Couple, Two Children	$9,828	$1,000	$4,613	$500	$641		$16,582
QUEBEC							
Single Employable[12]	$6,444				$210		$6,654
Person with a Disability[13]	$9,312				$253		$9,565
Single Parent, One Child[14]	$8,712		$2,633	$1,925	$531		$13,800
Couple, Two Children	$10,939	$199	$4,613	$1,250	$641		$17,642
ONTARIO							
Single Employable	$6,240				$210	$383	$6,833
Person with a Disability	$11,160				$297	$306	$11,763
Single Parent, One Child[15]	$10,210	$105	$2,633		$531	$393	$13,871
Couple, Two Children[16]	$12,223	$407	$4,613		$641	$516	$18,400

TABLE 1.2: ESTIMATED 2002 ANNUAL WELFARE INCOME BY TYPE OF HOUSEHOLD

	Basic Social Assistance	Additional Benefits	Federal Child Tax Benefit[1]	Provincial/ Territorial Child Benefits	Federal GST Credit[2]	Provincial/ Territorial Tax Credits	Total Income
MANITOBA							
Single Employable	$5,352				$210		$5,562
Person with a Disability[17]	$7,157	$960			$236		$8,353
Single Parent, One Child[18]	$9,636		$2,633		$531		$12,799
Couple, Two Children[19]	$12,849		$4,613		$641		$18,103
SASKATCHEWAN[20]							
Single Employable	$5,808				$210		$6,018
Person with a Disability	$7,416	$1,020			$241		$8,677
Single Parent, One Child[21]	$9,036		$2,633	$651	$531		$12,850
Couple, Two Children[22]	$12,192	$215	$4,613	$669	$641		$18,330
ALBERTA							
Single Employable	$4,764	$60			$210		$5,034
Person with a Disability	$6,384	$996			$221		$7,601
Single Parent, One Child[23]	$8,505	$60	$2,539		$531		$11,634
Couple, Two Children[24]	$12,678	$395	$4,698		$641		$18,412

TABLE 1.2: ESTIMATED 2002 ANNUAL WELFARE INCOME BY TYPE OF HOUSEHOLD

	Basic Social Assistance	Additional Benefits	Federal Child Tax Benefit[1]	Provincial/ Territorial Child Benefits	Federal GST Credit[2]	Provincial/ Territorial Tax Credits	Total Income
BRITISH COLUMBIA							
Single Employable[25]	$6,166	$35				$50	$6,461
Person with a Disability[26]	$9,437	$35			$210	$50	$9,784
Single Parent, One Child[27]	$10,300	$80	$2,633	$114	$262	$50	$13,706
Couple, Two Children[28]	$12,253	$190	$4,613	$430	$531	$100	$18,227
YUKON[29]					$641		
Single Employable	$11,990	$155			$304		$12,449
Person with a Disability	$11,990	$1,655			$321		$13,966
Single Parent, One Child[30]	$15,816	$548	$2,633	$300	$531		$19,827
Couple, Two Children[31]	$21,561	$685	$4,613	$0	$641		$27,500
NORTHWEST TERRITORIES [32]							
Single Employable	$11,490				$246		$11,736
Person with a Disability[33]	$14,830				$291		$15,121
Single Parent, One Child[34]	$18,050		$2,633	$330	$531		$21,543
Couple, Two Children[35]	$23,036		$4,613	$660	$641		$28,950

TABLE 1.2: ESTIMATED 2002 ANNUAL WELFARE INCOME BY TYPE OF HOUSEHOLD

	Basic Social Assistance	Additional Benefits	Federal Child Tax Benefit[1]	Provincial/ Territorial Child Benefits	Federal GST Credit[2]	Provincial/ Territorial Tax Credits	Total Income
NUNAVUT							
Single Employable[36]	$10,148				$278		$10,426
Person with a Disability	$12,288				$318		$12,606
Single Parent, One Child[37]	$24,802		$2,214	$330	$531		$27,877
Couple, Two Children	$28,431		$2,941	$660	$549		$32,582

[1] The federal child tax benefit includes the basic Canada Child Tax Benefit and the National Child Benefit Supplement that were received between January 1 and December 31, 2002.

[2] The federal GST credit includes the quarterly payments received between January 1 and December 31, 2002.

Newfoundland and Labrador

[3] An increase of one percent to room and board rates was effective July 1, 2001.

Prince Edward Island

[4] An increase to basic assistance and shelter was effective April 1, 2002.

[5] An increase to the personal comfort allowance was effective April 1, 2002.

[6] An increase to the healthy child allowance was effective August 1, 2002. PEI reduced the basic social assistance by the full amount of the National Child Benefit Supplement.

[7] An increase to the healthy child allowance was effective August 1, 2002. PEI reduced the basic social assistance by the full amount of the National Child Benefit Supplement.

Nova Scotia

[8] An increase to personal allowance and basic shelter was effective October 1, 2001.

[9] An increase to the shelter allowance was effective October 1, 2001.

[10] Nova Scotia eliminated personal allowances for children under 18 effective August 1, 2001. Nova Scotia no longer treats the National Child Benefit as non-exempt income effective August 1, 2001. An increase to the Nova Scotia Child Benefit was effective July 1, 2001.

[11] Nova Scotia eliminated personal allowances for children under 18 effective August 1, 2001. Nova Scotia no longer treats the National Child Benefit as non-exempt income effective August 1, 2001. An increase to the Nova Scotia Child Benefit was effective July 1, 2001.

Quebec

[12] An increase for applicants without a limited capacity for employment was effective January 1, 2002.

[13] An increase for applicants with a severely limited capacity for employment was effective January 1, 2002.

[14] An increase for applicants with a temporarily limited capacity for employment was effective January 1, 2002.

Ontario

[15] Ontario reduced basic social assistance by the full amount of the National Child Benefit Supplement. An increase in the provincial tax credit for the single parent with one child was effective in 2002.

[16] Ontario reduced basic social assistance by the full amount of the National Child Benefit Supplement. An increase in the provincial tax credit for the couple with two children was effective in 2002.

Manitoba

[17] An increase in the disabled benefit was effective for the full calendar year of 2002.

[18] A decrease in basic social assistance for the single parent with one child was effective July 2001. Manitoba no longer reduces basic social assistance by the National Child Benefit Supplement for children under seven effective July 1, 2001

[19] A decrease in basic social assistance for the additional allowance of $60 a month per household of two adults with children was effective January 2002. Manitoba reduced the basic social assistance by the full amount of the July 1999 rate of the National Child Benefit Supplement for children aged seven and over.

Saskatchewan

[20] An increase in utility rates is based upon actual average costs January to November 2002.

[21] The Saskatchewan Child Benefit was decreased by the full amount of the National Child Benefit Supplement. Saskatchewan also paid a Child Differential Allowance of $35 a month to the first child of a single parent.

[22] The Saskatchewan Child Benefit was decreased by the full amount of the National Child Benefit Supplement.

Alberta

[23] Alberta reduced basic social assistance by the full amount of the National Child Benefit Supplement. The federal government provided the same basic federal child tax benefit to eligible families in all provinces and territories. The one exception is Alberta which asked the federal government to adjust the benefit depending upon the age of the child.

[24] Alberta reduced basic social assistance by the full amount of the National Child Benefit Supplement. The federal government provided the same basic federal child tax benefit to eligible families in all provinces and territories. The one exception is Alberta which asked the federal government to adjust the benefit depending upon the age of the child.

British Columbia

[25] BC eliminated the once in a lifetime benefit in the first month of assistance for the single employable person effective April 1, 2002 which will take effect in 2003. The higher rate for persons aged 55 to 64 was also eliminated.

[26] Effective September 1, 2002, Disability Benefits II was replaced by Persons with Disabilities (PWD). DBII recipients are being reviewed under the new PWD eligibility criteria which may result in changes in 2003. The Disability I category was replaced by Persons with Persistent Multiple Barriers (PPMB) and may result in changes for these recipients in 2003.

[27] A decrease in basic social assistance for the single parent with one child was effective April 1, 2002. The Family Bonus is also reduced by the full amount of the National Child Benefit Supplement.

[28] A decrease in basic social assistance for the couple with two children was effective April 1, 2002. The Family Bonus is also reduced by the full amount of the National Child Benefit Supplement. A decrease in the shelter payment was also effective July 1, 2002.

Yukon

[29] An increase in fuel and utilities was effective February 1, 2001.

[30] The Yukon Child Benefit Program was introduced July 1, 1999 and is $300 per child per year if a family's income is less than $16,700 in the previous tax year. Yukon deducts two percent of income over $16,700 from the annual benefit for a single parent.

[31] The Yukon Child Benefit Program was introduced July 1, 1999 and is $300 per child per year if a family's income is less than $16,700 in the previous tax year. Yukon deducts five percent of income over $16,700 from the annual benefit of two-parent families. As a result, this family received no assistance from the program.

Northwest Territories

[32] An increase in food rates was effective September 1, 2001. An increase in shelter for single and disabled persons, clothing, and seasonal clothing was effective May 1, 2002.

[33] An increase in the disabled allowance was effective May 1, 2002.

[34] NWT reduced basic social assistance by the full amount of the National Child Benefit Supplement.

[35] NWT reduced basic social assistance by the full amount of the National Child Benefit Supplement.

Nunavut

[36] Nunavut paid a lower clothing allowance for the single employable applicant for the first two months of welfare.

[37] Nunavut reduced basic social assistance by the full amount of the National Child Benefit Supplement. Due to the higher welfare incomes of Nunavut families, the supplement was paid at a lower level than the standard payment to families in other provinces and territories.

II. ADEQUACY OF BENEFITS

The welfare incomes in Table 1.2 for 2002 have not improved from the abysmally low levels reported in previous years. To demonstrate this trend, we compared them with the estimated poverty line for 2002. The results are shown in Table 2.1.

Each year, Statistics Canada calculates the low income cut-offs or LICOs for households of different sizes in communities of different sizes. They approximate levels of gross income where people are forced to spend much of their income on food, shelter and clothing. The poverty lines in this report are estimated and brought up to date using the Consumer Price Index.

The National Council of Welfare regards the low income cut-offs as poverty lines. Like any poverty lines, they have their limitations, but they are widely accepted as a benchmark for judging income adequacy in Canada. Other studies of poverty, especially local surveys using a "market basket" approach, have produced comparable results. The National Council of Welfare's *Poverty Profile* series discusses the issue of poverty lines in more depth.

Some provincial governments maintain that the poverty lines are an especially imperfect measure of poverty when it comes to welfare incomes, because the lines are based on pre-tax income and welfare benefits are not taxable. In reality, most of the incomes in Table 2.1 are so low that there is little or no difference between taxable and non-taxable income. For example, single employable people in Newfoundland and Labrador with a total welfare income of $3,298 (including federal and provincial tax credits) were abysmally poor by any standard. Even if they had income of this amount from earnings, they would have been exempt from income tax because their earnings were so low.

Some provinces and territories also contend that welfare income is intended to provide only the bare necessities of life, while the incomes at the level of the low income cut-offs are high enough to allow some discretionary spending as well. The National Council of Welfare has no sympathy for that argument. The fact is that the cut-offs already represent very low levels of income. The only "discretion" many welfare recipients have is how to cut back on food when the money starts running short toward the end of the month.

As Table 2.1 shows, no province had welfare rates consistently closer to the poverty lines than elsewhere. Rates in some provinces, especially rates for single employables, are far below the lines. Welfare incomes which reach only one fifth or one third of the poverty line are unacceptably low and should be raised at the earliest possible date. Rates this low cannot be described as anything other than punitive and cruel.

Column one of Table 2.1 shows the total welfare incomes of four different types of households in the ten provinces in 2002. The three territories are not included in this table because they are specifically excluded from the survey used to generate the low income cut-offs.

Column two indicates the estimated 2002 poverty line (Statistics Canada's low income cut-offs, 1992 base) for the largest city in each province. The poverty gap, or difference between the total welfare income and the poverty line, is shown in column three. The fourth column represents the total welfare income as a percentage of the poverty line, that is, total welfare income divided by the poverty line.

Welfare incomes for single employable people remained by far the least adequate during 2002. The welfare income for this household type ranged from a low of 20 percent of the poverty line in Newfoundland and Labrador as well as in New Brunswick to a high of 36 percent of the poverty line in Prince Edward Island and Saskatchewan.

Welfare incomes for single people with disabilities were the lowest in Alberta at 39 percent of the poverty line followed by New Brunswick at 42 percent and Manitoba at 43 percent of the poverty line. The highest rate observed was in Ontario at 61 percent of the poverty line in 2002 down from 62 percent in 2001.

Welfare incomes for single-parent families were the lowest in Alberta at 48 percent of the poverty line followed by Manitoba at 53 percent of the poverty line. The highest rate was in Newfoundland and Labrador where welfare incomes for this household type was at 72 percent of the poverty line in 2002 down from 73 percent of the poverty line in 2001.

Finally, the welfare incomes for two-parent families with two children were the lowest in Quebec at 49 percent of the poverty line followed by Manitoba and British Colombia at 50 percent of the poverty line and Ontario and Alberta at 51 percent of the poverty line. The highest rate for this household type was in Prince Edward Island with a rate of 65 percent of the poverty line in 2002 up from 64 percent of the poverty line in 2001.

In 2002, welfare incomes ranged from a low of only one fifth of the estimated poverty line in Canada to a high of almost three quarters of the poverty line. The poverty gap has actually increased for all of our household types in Newfoundland, New Brunswick, Ontario, Alberta, and British Colombia compared to 2001. Only one province, Quebec, showed a narrowing of the poverty gap for three of the four household types.

TABLE 2.1: ADEQUACY OF 2002 BENEFITS				
	Total Welfare Income	Poverty Line	Poverty Gap	Total Welfare Income as % of Poverty Line
NEWFOUNDLAND AND LABRADOR				
Single Employable	$3,298	$16,516	-$13,218	20%
Person with a Disability	$8,925	$16,516	-$7,590	54%
Single Parent, One Child	$14,903	$20,644	-$5,741	72%
Couple, Two Children	$17,886	$31,080	-$13,194	58%
PRINCE EDWARD ISLAND				
Single Employable	$5,967	$16,401	-$10,434	36%
Person with a Disability	$8,956	$16,401	-$7,445	55%
Single Parent, One Child	$12,977	$20,501	-$7,524	63%
Couple, Two Children	$20,077	$30,864	-$10,787	65%
NOVA SCOTIA				
Single Employable	$5,190	$16,516	-$11,326	31%
Person with a Disability	$8,820	$16,516	-$7,695	53%
Single Parent, One Child	$12,368	$20,644	-$8,276	60%
Couple, Two Children	$17,864	$31,080	-$13,216	57%
NEW BRUNSWICK				
Single Employable	$3,378	$16,516	-$13,138	20%
Person with a Disability	$6,906	$16,516	-$9,610	42%
Single Parent, One Child	$13,085	$20,644	-$7,559	63%
Couple, Two Children	$16,582	$31,080	-$14,498	53%
QUEBEC				
Single Employable	$6,654	$19,256	-$12,602	35%
Person with a Disability	$9,565	$19,256	-$9,691	50%
Single Parent, One Child	$13,800	$24,069	-$10,269	57%
Couple, Two Children	$17,642	$36,235	-$18,593	49%

TABLE 2.1: ADEQUACY OF 2002 BENEFITS				
	Total Welfare Income	Poverty Line	Poverty Gap	Total Welfare Income as % of Poverty Line
ONTARIO				
Single Employable	$6,833	$19,256	-$12,422	35%
Person with a Disability	$11,763	$19,256	-$7,492	61%
Single Parent, One Child	$13,871	$24,069	-$10,198	58%
Couple, Two Children	$18,400	$36,235	-$17,835	51%
MANITOBA				
Single Employable	$5,562	$19,256	-$13,694	29%
Person with a Disability	$8,353	$19,256	-$10,903	43%
Single Parent, One Child	$12,799	$24,069	-$11,270	53%
Couple, Two Children	$18,103	$36,235	-$18,132	50%
SASKATCHEWAN				
Single Employable	$6,018	$16,516	-$10,498	36%
Person with a Disability	$8,677	$16,516	-$7,839	53%
Single Parent, One Child	$12,850	$20,644	-$7,794	62%
Couple, Two Children	$18,330	$31,080	-$12,750	59%
ALBERTA				
Single Employable	$5,034	$19,256	-$14,222	26%
Person with a Disability	$7,601	$19,256	-$11,654	39%
Single Parent, One Child	$11,634	$24,069	-$12,435	48%
Couple, Two Children	$18,412	$36,235	-$17,823	51%
BRITISH COLUMBIA				
Single Employable	$6,461	$19,256	-$12,795	34%
Person with a Disability	$9,784	$19,256	-$9,471	51%
Single Parent, One Child	$13,706	$24,069	-$10,363	57%
Couple, Two Children	$18,227	$36,235	-$18,008	50%

III. WELFARE AND AVERAGE INCOMES

The low level of financial support provided by social assistance is also evident when measured against total average incomes. Welfare provides only a portion of the level of income that most Canadians would consider normal or reasonable.

Table 3.1 compares the welfare incomes of our four typical households with average incomes for the appropriate household type in each province. The averages for 2002 are based on data collected by Statistics Canada in the Survey of Labour and Income Dynamics, inflated by the Consumer Price Index.

For the single employable person and the single person with a disability, we used average incomes in each province for unattached people under the age of 65. For single parents, we used the average incomes of single parents under 65 with children under 18. For the two-parent family, we used the average incomes of couples under 65 with children under 18.

Welfare incomes remain far, far below average. In 2002, the welfare income of a single employable person ranged in value from 15 percent of the average income of other single people in Newfoundland or New Brunswick to a high of 26 percent of the average incomes of single Prince Edward Islanders.

The welfare income of a disabled person ranged from a low of 25 percent of the income of other single Albertans, to 41 percent of the average income of other single Newfoundlanders. The single parent in Alberta received 27 percent of the average income of other single parents in that province, while a single parent on welfare in Newfoundland received 54 percent of the average income of other single parents in the province.

The couple with two children on welfare in Ontario received only 20 percent – one fifth – of the average income of other Ontario families of the same size. The best a two-parent family on welfare did was 33 percent – only one third – of the average incomes of other two-parent families in Prince Edward Island.

TABLE 3.1: 2002 WELFARE INCOMES AS PERCENTAGE OF AVERAGE INCOMES

	Welfare Income	Estimated Average Income	Welfare Income as % of Estimated Average Income
NEWFOUNDLAND AND LABRADOR			
Single Employable	$3,298	$21,744	15%
Person with a Disability	$8,925	$21,744	41%
Single Parent, One Child	$14,903	$27,534	54%
Couple, Two Children	$17,886	$60,449	30%
PRINCE EDWARD ISLAND			
Single Employable	$5,967	$22,960	26%
Person with a Disability	$8,956	$22,960	39%
Single Parent, One Child	$12,977	$35,185	37%
Couple, Two Children	$20,077	$60,583	33%
NOVA SCOTIA			
Single Employable	$5,190	$24,426	21%
Person with a Disability	$8,820	$24,426	36%
Single Parent, One Child	$12,368	$31,468	39%
Couple, Two Children	$17,864	$67,205	27%
NEW BRUNSWICK			
Single Employable	$3,378	$22,478	15%
Person with a Disability	$6,906	$22,478	31%
Single Parent, One Child	$13,085	$30,547	43%
Couple, Two Children	$16,582	$64,273	26%
QUEBEC			
Single Employable	$6,654	$28,798	23%
Person with a Disability	$9,565	$28,798	33%
Single Parent, One Child	$13,800	$33,275	41%
Couple, Two Children	$17,642	$73,887	24%

TABLE 3.1: 2002 WELFARE INCOMES AS PERCENTAGE OF AVERAGE INCOMES			
	Welfare Income	Estimated Average Income	Welfare Income as % of Estimated Average Income
ONTARIO			
Single Employable	$6,833	$35,267	19%
Person with a Disability	$11,763	$35,267	33%
Single Parent, One Child	$13,871	$41,787	33%
Couple, Two Children	$18,400	$90,606	20%
MANITOBA			
Single Employable	$5,562	$29,656	19%
Person with a Disability	$8,353	$29,656	28%
Single Parent, One Child	$12,799	$31,913	40%
Couple, Two Children	$18,103	$67,285	27%
SASKATCHEWAN			
Single Employable	$6,018	$27,633	22%
Person with a Disability	$8,677	$27,633	31%
Single Parent, One Child	$12,850	$29,239	44%
Couple, Two Children	$18,330	$70,960	26%
ALBERTA			
Single Employable	$5,034	$30,664	16%
Person with a Disability	$7,601	$30,664	25%
Single Parent, One Child	$11,634	$43,098	27%
Couple, Two Children	$18,412	$81,001	23%
BRITISH COLUMBIA			
Single Employable	$6,461	$32,593	20%
Person with a Disability	$9,784	$32,593	30%
Single Parent, One Child	$13,706	$36,117	38%
Couple, Two Children	$18,227	$77,910	23%

IV. PROVINCIAL AND TERRITORIAL BENEFITS OVER TIME

No other program of income support is as erratic as welfare. Every year, there are gains and losses that vary from one category of recipient to another and one jurisdiction to another. Tables 4.1 and 4.2 summarize the ups and downs of recent years, taking into consideration the impact of inflation.

The figures consist of those benefits shown in Table 1.2 that are exclusively within provincial and territorial jurisdiction, in other words, total welfare incomes less the National Child Benefit and the GST credit. Comparable figures for other years were calculated from *Welfare in Canada: The Tangled Safety Net* and previous editions of *Welfare Incomes*.

Using the Consumer Price Index, all the dollar figures in Table 4.1 are expressed in constant 2002 dollars to factor out the effects of inflation and to show the real purchasing power of welfare benefits over time. The percentages in the three columns of Table 4.2 show increases or decreases in real purchasing power over time.

The tables provide comparisons of provincial and territorial benefits from 1986 to 2002 for the single employable person, the single-parent family and the two-parent family. The National Council of Welfare did not include the single person with a disability in its original calculations of welfare incomes for 1986, so the comparison for this group is available from 1989 to 2002. The National Council of Welfare first estimated welfare incomes in Northwest Territories in 1993, so the table shows comparisons only since that time. The data for Nunavut begin in 1999 when the territory was created.

Most welfare recipients in Canada saw a further erosion of their welfare incomes in 2002. Between 2001 and 2002, the cost of living rose by 2.2 percent. Provincial and territorial welfare benefits decreased, were frozen, or increased only slightly in most jurisdictions. When the change from 2001 to 2002 appears as -2.2 percent, it means that the welfare rates were frozen and welfare recipients lost 2.2 percent of their purchasing power to inflation.

Between 2001 and 2002, the purchasing power of welfare benefits dropped in every jurisdiction with the exception of Quebec and Northwest Territories. In Newfoundland and Labrador, the welfare income of the single employable person dropped by 1.6 percent. The disabled single person, single parent with a two year old, and the couple with a 10 and 15 year old all experienced a drop in the value of their provincial welfare benefits of 1.9 percent.

In Prince Edward Island, the value of provincial welfare incomes decreased for the single employable, single disabled, and couple with two children by 0.1 percent. The province increased welfare for the disabled in April, but not enough to outpace the increasing cost of living. For the single parent with a two year old, the value of welfare increased by 0.4 percent due to the increase in the Healthy Child Allowance and the increases to provincial welfare.

In Nova Scotia, the value of welfare increased for the single employable and single disabled person by 5.7 and 4.1 percent respectively. The province increased personal and shelter allowances at a rate higher than the cost of living for these two household types. The value of provincial welfare decreased for the single parent with one child by three percent and decreased for the couple with a 10 and 15 year old by 8.4 percent. Nova Scotia eliminated personal allowances for children on welfare in August 2001. Increases in adult personal allowances and shelter were still insufficient to compensate for this loss in welfare income and the cost of living. Families on welfare in Nova Scotia lost a great deal in terms of real dollars over this period.

In New Brunswick, the single employable person, disabled single person, single parent with a two year old, and the couple with a 10 and 15 year old all experienced drops in the value of their welfare by 2.2 percent. This matches the change in the cost of living because New Brunswick welfare rates were frozen.

In Quebec, all family types had a slight increase in the value of their incomes due to a slight increase in provincial welfare benefits. Benefits for the single employable person rose by 1.6 percent. Benefits for the disabled single person and single parent with a two year old rose by half a percent. The couple with two children experienced an increase in the value of their welfare benefits by 0.7 percent.

In Ontario, all four household types experienced a loss in the purchasing power of their welfare benefits. Benefits for the single employable and single disabled person dropped by 2.2 percent or the 2002 cost of living because the province froze their welfare payments. Provincial benefits for the single parent with one child dropped by 3.5 percent and the couple with two children lost 4.4 percent. The larger drop in provincial government income for the two families with children occurs because of the clawback of the supplement to the federal child tax benefit.

In Manitoba, single employable and single disabled recipients saw their welfare benefits depreciate by 2.2 percent. This reflects the provincial government's freeze on benefits, and on the loss of the cost of living. The single parent with a two year old saw a very slight increase of 0.7 percent which reflects Manitoba's decision to cease its clawback of the supplement to the federal child tax benefit for children under seven. The couple with two older children saw a decrease in the value of their benefits drop by 2.1 percent. This decrease is slightly less than the cost of living. This is because the province deducted slightly less than the full value of the supplement to the federal child benefit.

In Saskatchewan, the single parent saw a slight increase in the value of welfare benefits by 0.8 percent. This was the only Saskatchewan family type to see an increase in provincial welfare. Welfare for the single employable person decreased by 1.5 percent. The single disabled person saw a decrease by two percent, and the couple with a 10 and 15 year old saw their benefits depreciate by 4.0 percent. Saskatchewan increased its utility rates for all household types which almost offset the cost of living. However, the couple with older children suffered from a larger reduction of the provincial child benefit program.

In Alberta, the single employable and single disabled person saw a decrease by the cost of living. The single parent with a two year old and the couple with a 10 and 15 year old saw losses of 4.1 and 4.7 percent due to decreases in provincial welfare payments equal to the value of the federal government's supplement to the child tax benefit.

In British Columbia, the single and single disabled person saw losses equal to the cost of living. For the single parent with a two year old, the loss was 7.1 percent and for the couple with two children, 6.2 percent, reflecting the provincial government's clawback of the supplement to the federal child tax benefit.

In Yukon, the value of welfare benefits decreased for all of the household types. The single employable person saw a loss of 1.3 percent, the disabled person saw a loss of 1.4 percent, the single parent saw a loss of 2.6 percent, and the couple saw a loss of 4.7 percent. Yukon increased its allowance for heating for all household types. For the families with children, the clawback of their provincial benefits by the amount of the federal child tax benefit supplement resulted in losses in their provincial welfare income.

In Northwest Territories, all household types saw an increase in the value of their benefits. For the single employable and disabled persons, the increases were substantial at 28.8 percent and 30.8 percent. These increases were due to increases across the board for food, shelter, and clothing that took effect in the autumn of 2001. For the single parent and couple households the increases were minor at 0.9 percent and 0.7 percent as the large gains in general welfare payments were offset by the clawback of the supplement to the federal child tax benefit.

In Nunavut, all household types experienced a slight decrease. Nunavut reduced the clothing allowance for single employable people when they first started on welfare. This change and the cost of living caused a drop in value by 2.5 percent. Benefits for the disabled person were frozen, so they dropped in value by the cost of living. Nunavut reduced its contribution to the income of the two families on welfare by clawing back the value of the supplement to the federal child tax benefit. The supplement to the federal child benefit is slightly less than the supplement to families in other jurisdictions due to higher family incomes on welfare in the territory. As a result, the territorial clawback is also slightly smaller.

TABLE 4.1: PROVINCIAL AND TERRITORIAL WELFARE BENEFITS IN 2002 CONSTANT DOLLARS

	1986	1989	1990	1991	1992	1993	1994	1995	1996	1997	1998	1999	2000	2001	2002
NEWFOUNDLAND AND LABRADOR															
Single Employable	5,165	4,982	4,952	4,875	5,118	5,057	5,048	4,940	2,812	1,225	1,232	1,230	1,715	3,138	3,088
Person with a Disability		10,036	9,930	9,630	9,845	9,714	9,698	9,490	9,340	9,261	9,215	9,133	8,996	8,846	8,680
Single Parent, One Child	12,948	12,683	12,658	12,800	13,326	13,165	13,143	12,861	12,658	12,564	12,534	12,387	12,159	11,961	11,740
Couple, Two Children	14,978	14,672	14,637	14,167	14,422	14,245	14,221	13,916	13,697	13,724	13,674	13,440	13,087	12,873	12,632
PRINCE EDWARD ISLAND															
Single Employable	9,592	9,281	9,237	9,234	9,368	9,301	8,356	6,435	5,895	5,879	5,826	5,725	5,867	5,764	5,757
Person with a Disability		10,802	10,691	10,539	10,667	10,577	10,447	10,047	9,263	9,078	8,996	8,840	8,898	8,720	8,712
Single Parent, One Child	13,222	12,795	12,894	12,793	12,995	12,920	12,674	12,064	11,512	11,029	10,598	9,991	10,056	9,774	9,814
Couple, Two Children	19,376	19,058	19,054	19,165	19,401	19,255	18,886	18,116	16,717	16,757	16,052	15,036	15,327	14,840	14,823
NOVA SCOTIA															
Single Employable	7,050	7,862	7,500	7,132	7,026	6,902	6,890	6,742	6,656	4,897	4,853	4,711	4,584	4,712	4,980
Person with a Disability		10,348	10,282	10,133	9,996	9,820	9,971	9,785	9,630	9,476	9,391	9,228	8,979	8,244	8,580
Single Parent, One Child	12,209	12,578	12,485	12,336	12,338	12,120	12,292	12,060	11,869	11,679	11,379	10,934	10,524	9,488	9,205
Couple, Two Children	14,696	16,001	15,287	14,776	14,794	14,580	14,555	14,243	15,289	15,475	15,011	13,780	13,478	13,771	12,610

...ND TERRITORIAL WELFARE BENEFITS IN 2002 CONSTANT DOLLARS

	1986	1989	1990	1991	1992	1993	1994	1995	1996	1997	1998	1999	2000	2001	2002
...ICK															
...oyable	3,475	3,760	3,703	3,624	3,627	3,577	3,599	3,536	3,520	3,504	3,472	3,412	3,320	3,238	3,168
...with a Disability		9,851	9,695	9,413	9,425	9,366	7,347	7,318	7,287	7,369	7,339	7,212	7,017	6,843	6,696
Single Parent, One Child	10,436	10,193	10,032	9,809	9,882	9,913	10,321	10,822	10,760	10,883	10,877	10,688	10,398	10,140	9,922
Couple, Two Children	11,290	11,028	10,838	10,737	11,088	11,120	11,525	12,114	12,039	12,347	12,420	12,205	11,872	11,577	11,328
QUEBEC															
Single Employable	3,658	4,700	6,667	6,924	7,133	7,154	7,002	6,852	6,744	6,536	6,444	6,488	6,372	6,346	6,444
Person with a Disability		8,449	8,762	9,012	9,289	9,287	9,439	9,236	9,293	9,277	9,364	9,383	9,269	9,264	9,312
Single Parent, One Child	12,308	11,418	12,164	11,132	12,641	13,168	13,453	13,165	12,957	12,267	11,862	11,353	10,784	10,579	10,637
Couple, Two Children	15,908	14,912	14,587	15,017	15,530	15,992	15,783	15,445	15,201	14,416	13,909	13,120	12,562	12,306	12,388
ONTARIO															
Single Employable	7,817	8,404	9,174	9,415	9,741	9,710	9,716	9,019	7,400	7,325	7,259	7,133	6,941	6,769	6,623
Person with a Disability		12,135	12,941	13,228	13,449	13,373	13,381	13,094	12,888	12,682	12,567	12,349	12,017	11,718	11,466
Single Parent, One Child	13,999	15,083	16,898	17,314	17,632	17,606	17,619	16,338	13,421	13,230	12,776	12,139	11,625	11,100	10,708
Couple, Two Children	17,425	19,034	22,171	22,586	23,081	23,023	22,829	21,038	17,341	17,097	16,380	15,369	14,583	13,748	13,146

TABLE 4.1: PROVINCIAL AND TERRITORIAL WELFARE BENEFITS IN 2002 CONSTANT DOLLARS

	1986	1989	1990	1991	1992	1993	1994	1995	1996	1997	1998	1999	2000	2001	2002
MANITOBA															
Single Employable	7,756	8,047	8,150	8,053	8,218	8,085	7,526	7,375	6,823	5,919	5,866	5,764	5,609	5,470	5,352
Person with a Disability		8,751	8,634	8,492	10,443	9,406	9,332	9,132	8,989	8,845	8,764	8,688	8,506	8,295	8,117
Single Parent, One Child	11,982	11,744	11,599	11,406	12,635	11,336	11,245	11,004	10,831	10,657	10,229	9,629	9,402	9,569	9,636
Couple, Two Children	18,154	19,060	20,501	20,511	21,112	19,249	19,587	19,156	17,167	15,873	14,984	13,987	13,463	13,129	12,849
SASKATCHEWAN															
Single Employable	6,492	6,498	6,350	6,161	6,396	6,733	6,722	6,578	6,474	5,831	5,796	5,966	5,921	5,899	5,808
Person with a Disability		10,589	10,251	9,857	9,770	9,679	9,663	9,456	9,576	8,557	8,560	8,788	8,654	8,609	8,436
Single Parent, One Child	13,321	13,272	12,890	12,410	12,270	12,135	12,115	11,856	11,668	11,482	10,179	10,213	9,908	9,608	9,687
Couple, Two Children	18,687	18,416	17,876	17,185	17,473	17,235	17,272	16,905	16,639	15,418	14,837	14,811	14,109	13,625	13,076
ALBERTA															
Single Employable	9,238	6,422	6,124	6,661	6,712	6,327	5,518	5,399	5,314	5,260	5,287	5,195	5,056	4,930	4,824
Person with a Disability		7,942	7,574	7,976	7,925	7,694	7,665	7,523	7,405	7,317	7,326	7,386	7,734	7,542	7,380
Single Parent, One Child	13,527	12,041	11,483	12,052	12,024	11,545	10,727	10,497	10,331	10,250	10,066	9,778	9,398	8,933	8,565
Children	20,112	17,741	16,918	18,654	18,678	17,991	16,889	16,698	16,435	16,249	15,855	15,061	14,538	13,720	13,073

TABLE 4.1: PROVINCIAL AND TERRITORIAL WELFARE BENEFITS IN 2002 CONSTANT DOLLARS

	1986	1989	1990	1991	1992	1993	1994	1995	1996	1997	1998	1999	2000	2001	2002
BRITISH COLUMBIA															
Single Employable	6,599	7,241	7,400	7,284	7,507	7,532	7,720	7,579	6,891	6,781	6,720	6,603	6,478	6,389	6,251
Person with a Disability		9,993	10,333	10,096	10,539	10,611	10,859	10,663	10,495	10,327	10,233	10,056	9,866	9,732	9,522
Single Parent, One Child	11,884	13,081	13,214	12,951	13,534	13,583	13,918	13,663	13,448	13,177	12,726	12,096	11,691	11,347	10,543
Couple, Two Children	16,232	16,338	16,445	16,068	17,123	17,225	17,748	17,425	17,150	16,765	16,060	15,069	14,412	13,831	12,973
YUKON															
Single Employable	7,841	9,467	9,577	9,421	9,395	9,229	9,213	9,016	8,874	12,105	11,996	11,788	11,470	12,310	12,145
Person with a Disability		10,590	10,648	10,436	10,395	10,211	10,194	10,729	10,560	13,764	13,640	13,403	13,042	13,843	13,645
Single Parent, One Child	14,082	15,648	15,739	15,607	15,603	15,328	15,302	14,974	14,738	18,210	17,714	17,307	16,646	17,117	16,664
Couple, Two Children	21,575	23,491	23,325	23,328	23,520	23,105	23,066	22,572	22,216	26,229	25,438	24,259	23,238	23,343	22,246
NORTHWEST TERRITORIES															
Single Employable						13,214	13,192	12,909	12,621	7,963	8,176	9,153	8,907	8,923	11,490
Person with a Disability						14,968	14,942	14,622	14,645	10,551	10,522	11,458	11,149	11,335	14,830
Single Parent, One Child						22,403	22,364	21,885	21,439	18,753	18,554	19,516	18,795	18,216	18,380
Couple, Two Children						26,513	26,510	25,942	25,398	25,155	25,178	25,603	24,527	23,528	23,696
NUNAVUT															
Single Employable												10,972	10,677	10,412	10,148
Person with a Disability												13,234	12,878	12,558	12,288
Single Parent, One Child												27,691	26,750	25,846	25,132
Couple, Two Children												32,747	31,479	30,217	29,091

TABLE 4.2: CHANGE IN PERCENTAGE OF PROVINCIAL AND TERRITORIAL WELFARE BENEFITS IN 2002 CONSTANT DOLLARS

	% Change 1986-2002	% Change 1989-2002	% Change 2001-2002		% Change 1986-2002	% Change 1989-2002	% Change 2001-2002
NEWFOUNDLAND AND LABRADOR				**PRINCE EDWARD ISLAND**			
Single Employable	-40.2%	-38.0%	-1.6%	Single Employable	-40.0%	-38.0%	-0.1%
Person with a Disability		-13.5%	-1.9%	Person with a Disability		-19.3%	-0.1%
Single Parent, One Child	-9.3%	-7.4%	-1.9%	Single Parent, One Child	-25.8%	-23.3%	0.4%
Couple, Two Children	-15.7%	-13.9%	-1.9%	Couple, Two Children	-23.5%	-22.2%	-0.1%
NOVA SCOTIA				**NEW BRUNSWICK**			
Single Employable	-29.4%	-36.7%	5.7%	Single Employable	-8.8%	-15.7%	-2.2%
Person with a Disability		-17.1%	4.1%	Person with a Disability		-32.0%	-2.2%
Single Parent, One Child	-24.6%	-26.8%	-3.0%	Single Parent, One Child	-4.9%	-2.7%	-2.2%
Couple, Two Children	-14.2%	-21.2%	-8.4%	Couple, Two Children	0.3%	2.7%	-2.2%
QUEBEC				**ONTARIO**			
Single Employable	76.2%	37.1%	1.6%	Single Employable	-15.3%	-21.2%	-2.2%
Person with a Disability		10.2%	0.5%	Person with a Disability		-5.5%	-2.2%
Single Parent, One Child	-13.6%	-6.8%	0.5%	Single Parent, One Child	-23.5%	-29.0%	-3.5%
Couple, Two Children	-22.1%	-16.9%	0.7%	Couple, Two Children	-24.6%	-30.9%	-4.4%
MANITOBA				**SASKATCHEWAN**			
Single Employable	-31.0%	-33.5%	-2.2%	Single Employable	-10.5%	-10.6%	-1.5%
Person with a Disability		-7.2%	-2.2%	Person with a Disability		-20.3%	-2.0%
Single Parent, One Child	-19.6%	-18.0%	0.7%	Single Parent, One Child	-27.3%	-27.0%	0.8%
Couple, Two Children	-29.2%	-32.6%	-2.1%	Couple, Two Children	-30.0%	-29.0%	-4.0%

TABLE 4.2: CHANGE IN PERCENTAGE OF PROVINCIAL AND TERRITORIAL WELFARE BENEFITS IN 2002 CONSTANT DOLLARS

	% Change 1986-2002	% Change 1989-2002	% Change 2001-2002
ALBERTA			
Single Employable	-47.8%	-24.9%	-2.2%
Person with a Disability		-7.1%	-2.2%
Single Parent, One Child	-36.7%	-28.9%	-4.1%
Couple, Two Children	-35.0%	-26.3%	-4.7%
YUKON			
Single Employable	54.9%	28.3%	-1.3%
Person with a Disability		28.8%	-1.4%
Single Parent, One Child	18.3%	6.5%	-2.6%
Couple, Two Children	3.1%	-5.3%	-4.7%
NUNAVUT			
Single Employable			-2.5%
Person with a Disability			-2.2%
Single Parent, One Child			-2.8%
Couple, Two Children			-3.7%

	% Change 1986-2002	% Change 1989-2002	% Change 2001-2002
BRITISH COLUMBIA			
Single Employable	-5.3%	-13.7%	-2.2%
Person with a Disability		-4.7%	-2.2%
Single Parent, One Child	-11.3%	-19.4%	-7.1%
Couple, Two Children	-20.1%	-20.6%	-6.2%
NORTHWEST TERRITORIES			
Single Employable			28.8%
Person with a Disability			30.8%
Single Parent, One Child			0.9%
Couple, Two Children			0.7%

Most perverse of all the changes in provincial and territorial contributions to welfare incomes is the effect of the National Child Benefit. When the federal government introduced the National Child Benefit in 1998, it allowed provincial and territorial governments to claw back the supplement to the benefit by reducing the welfare benefits of families by the value of the supplement. Only Newfoundland and New Brunswick refused to exercise this option. Several other jurisdictions have since ceased to claw back later increases to the supplement. The charts at the end of this section show the effect of the clawback on the total welfare income of a single-parent family with one child and on a couple with two children.

There are two charts for each province and territory. One chart shows the total welfare income for the single parent with a two year old child and the other chart shows the total welfare income for the couple with a 10 and 15 year old. Each chart has a white bar that shows the contribution of the provincial or territorial government. The black bar shows the federal government contribution to welfare. The federal amount includes the GST, the basic federal child tax benefit and the supplement. We have calculated these welfare incomes over time by adjusting the amounts to the cost of living as we did in Tables 4.1 and 4.2. All the annual welfare incomes are expressed in 2002 constant dollars.

Together, the white and black bars show the total welfare income for the single-parent family with one child and the two-parent family with two children for the period since the National Council of Welfare began calculating welfare incomes in 1986. What these graphs show is that in those provinces and territories where the governments have clawed back the supplement to the federal child tax benefit, the federal government is providing a larger and larger share of welfare incomes, but the total welfare incomes of families with children have not improved. With only a few exceptions, the white bars that show the share of welfare incomes that is paid by the provinces and the territories become smaller as the years go on.

In Newfoundland and Labrador, Figure 4.1 shows that the total 2002 welfare income was $14,903 for the single parent with one child. This was made up of a contribution of $11,740 from the province and $3,163 from the federal government. When the cost of living is taken into account, single parents in Newfoundland and Labrador experienced a loss of $90 since 2001. The purchasing power of the welfare income of the single-parent family in Newfoundland and Labrador peaked in 1992 at $15,345. Even with the introduction of the federal child tax benefit supplement in 1998, the income of the single-parent family is below its 1992 peak of $15,345.

Figure 4.2 shows that the couple with two children had a total annual income of $17,886 in 2002 which consisted of $12,632 from the province and $5,254 from the federal government. The increase of $28 in total welfare income from 2001 is because of the increase in the federal government's supplement to the basic federal child tax benefit which the province does not claw back.

In Prince Edward Island, Figure 4.3 shows that the 2002 total welfare income of the single parent with one child was $12,977. This consisted of $9,814 from the provincial government and $3,163 from the federal government. This represented a slight increase from 2001 due to increases in provincial benefits that outpaced the province's clawback of the federal child supplement. The couple with two children in PEI also experienced a slight increase in the purchasing power of their total welfare income of $20,077 in 2002 but its income has not returned to its 1986 peak of $22,616.

In Nova Scotia, both the single parent and the couple experienced a drop in the value of their welfare incomes from 2001. Nova Scotia's cuts to personal allowances for children in August 2001 were greater than any benefit to families from the provincial government's decision to cease the claw back of the federal child supplement. For the single-parent family, the 2001 welfare income was worth $12,520, and dropped to $12,369 in 2002. The couple with two children saw their income drop from $18,756 in 2001 to $17,864 in 2002.

Families on welfare in New Brunswick saw relatively little change in the value of the welfare incomes. Welfare payments rates stayed the same, so they decreased in value by the cost of living. However, since the provincial government does not claw back the supplement to the federal child benefit, total welfare incomes were protected. The single parent lost $87 and the two-parent family gained $20 between 2001 and 2002.

Figures 4.9 and 4.10 show that the value of the Quebec families' welfare incomes increased slightly. The province increased basic welfare rates and decided not to claw back the supplement to the federal child benefit as of July 2001.

In Ontario, total welfare incomes for both family types have dropped steadily since Ontario cut welfare drastically in 1994. The federal portion of welfare incomes has grown since federal child benefits were introduced in 1998. However, Ontario's decision to claw back the supplement ensured that welfare families do not enjoy any improvement in benefits.

Manitoba decided to cease the clawback to the supplement for children under seven. As a result, the single-parent family experienced a slight increase in its total welfare income from both the provincial and the federal government. The couple with two children saw a slight drop in total welfare income as the province continued to claw back their federal child supplement.

In Saskatchewan, the single-parent family saw a slight increase in total welfare income as a result of increases to provincial benefits and the federal government's contribution to child benefits. The couple experienced a slight decrease in their total income because the provincial government froze their basic welfare benefits and clawed back the supplement to the federal child benefit.

Figures 4.17 and 4.18 show that the value of total welfare incomes in Alberta for the single-parent family dropped by $241 between 2001 and 2002, entirely because of provincial government clawbacks and cuts. The federal government actually increased its contribution to the income of this family from $2,941 in 2001 to $3,069 in 2002. The couple with two children saw their income drop by $387, again because of the provincial government's policies, and again, despite an increase in the federal government's contribution.

British Columbia decreased its welfare rates. BC also clawed back the supplement to the federal child benefit by reducing the BC Family Bonus. In constant dollars, the value of welfare for BC families peaked in 1994 and has dropped ever since. The value of the single-parent family's income was $13,706 in 2002, down $672 from 2001, even though the federal government gave this family more money. Similarly, the 2002 income for the two-parent family was $18,227, down $590 from the 2001 income. This occurred even as the federal government gave this family $269 more.

In Yukon, both family types experienced a drop in their total welfare income. Yukon clawed back the supplement to the federal child benefit while it froze welfare incomes. The value of welfare incomes peaked in 1997 for both families but have been in decline ever since. The single-parent family received $19,827 in 2002, down from $20,149 in 2001, and the two-parent family received $828 less in 2002 than it did in 2001.

In Northwest Territories, total welfare incomes for families increased slightly because of increases to basic welfare rates. NWT claws back the value of the supplement to the federal child tax benefit, but between 2001 and 2002 the increases to welfare were greater than the clawback.

Nunavut claws back the supplement to the federal child benefit by cutting welfare to families. As a result, in the three years since the territory was established, total welfare incomes for both family types shrunk. At the same time, the portion of welfare incomes supplied by the federal government has increased.

Figure 4.1: Newfoundland & Labrador Welfare Income, Single Parent, One Child (2002 dollars)

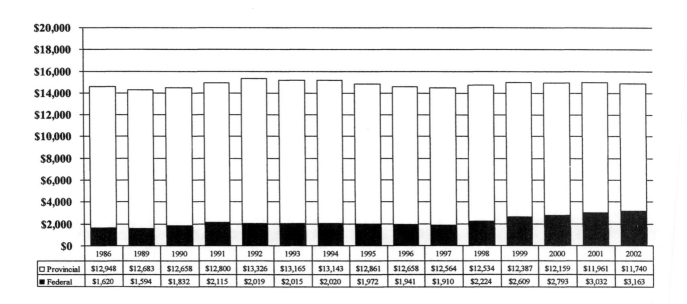

	1986	1989	1990	1991	1992	1993	1994	1995	1996	1997	1998	1999	2000	2001	2002
☐ Provincial	$12,948	$12,683	$12,658	$12,800	$13,326	$13,165	$13,143	$12,861	$12,658	$12,564	$12,534	$12,387	$12,159	$11,961	$11,740
■ Federal	$1,620	$1,594	$1,832	$2,115	$2,019	$2,015	$2,020	$1,972	$1,941	$1,910	$2,224	$2,609	$2,793	$3,032	$3,163

Figure 4.2: Newfoundland & Labrador Welfare Income, Couple, Two Children (2002 dollars)

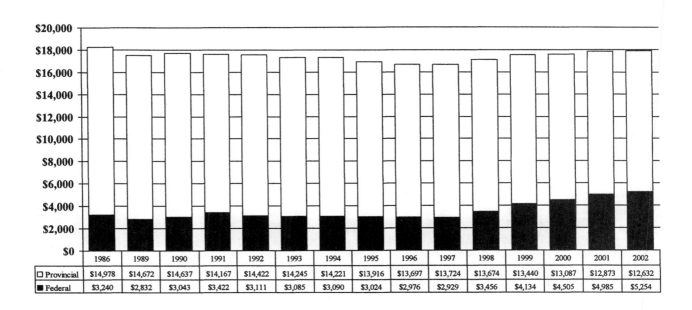

	1986	1989	1990	1991	1992	1993	1994	1995	1996	1997	1998	1999	2000	2001	2002
☐ Provincial	$14,978	$14,672	$14,637	$14,167	$14,422	$14,245	$14,221	$13,916	$13,697	$13,724	$13,674	$13,440	$13,087	$12,873	$12,632
■ Federal	$3,240	$2,832	$3,043	$3,422	$3,111	$3,085	$3,090	$3,024	$2,976	$2,929	$3,456	$4,134	$4,505	$4,985	$5,254

Figure 4.3: Prince Edward Island Welfare Income, Single Parent, One Child (2002 dollars)

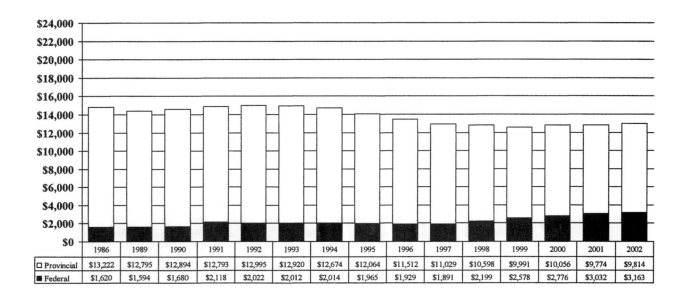

	1986	1989	1990	1991	1992	1993	1994	1995	1996	1997	1998	1999	2000	2001	2002
□ Provincial	$13,222	$12,795	$12,894	$12,793	$12,995	$12,920	$12,674	$12,064	$11,512	$11,029	$10,598	$9,991	$10,056	$9,774	$9,814
■ Federal	$1,620	$1,594	$1,680	$2,118	$2,022	$2,012	$2,014	$1,965	$1,929	$1,891	$2,199	$2,578	$2,776	$3,032	$3,163

Figure 4.4: Prince Edward Island Welfare Income, Couple, Two Children (2002 dollars)

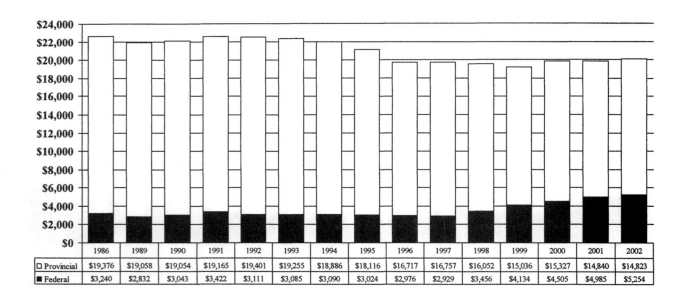

	1986	1989	1990	1991	1992	1993	1994	1995	1996	1997	1998	1999	2000	2001	2002
□ Provincial	$19,376	$19,058	$19,054	$19,165	$19,401	$19,255	$18,886	$18,116	$16,717	$16,757	$16,052	$15,036	$15,327	$14,840	$14,823
■ Federal	$3,240	$2,832	$3,043	$3,422	$3,111	$3,085	$3,090	$3,024	$2,976	$2,929	$3,456	$4,134	$4,505	$4,985	$5,254

NATIONAL COUNCIL OF WELFARE

Figure 4.5: Nova Scotia Welfare Income, Single Parent, One Child (2002 dollars)

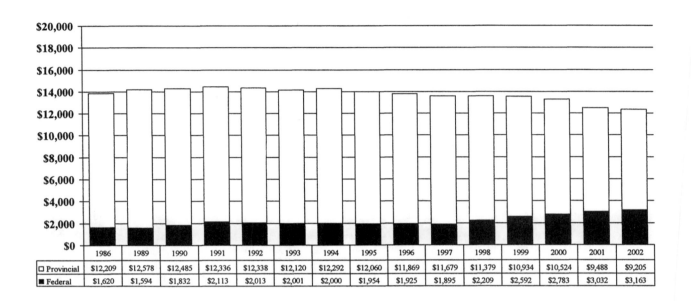

	1986	1989	1990	1991	1992	1993	1994	1995	1996	1997	1998	1999	2000	2001	2002
☐ Provincial	$12,209	$12,578	$12,485	$12,336	$12,338	$12,120	$12,292	$12,060	$11,869	$11,679	$11,379	$10,934	$10,524	$9,488	$9,205
■ Federal	$1,620	$1,594	$1,832	$2,113	$2,013	$2,001	$2,000	$1,954	$1,925	$1,895	$2,209	$2,592	$2,783	$3,032	$3,163

Figure 4.6: Nova Scotia Welfare Income, Couple, Two Children (2002 dollars)

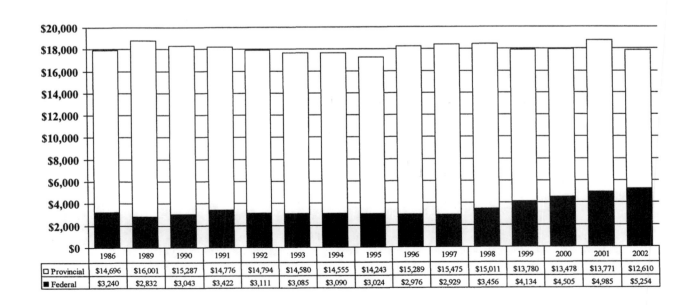

	1986	1989	1990	1991	1992	1993	1994	1995	1996	1997	1998	1999	2000	2001	2002
☐ Provincial	$14,696	$16,001	$15,287	$14,776	$14,794	$14,580	$14,555	$14,243	$15,289	$15,475	$15,011	$13,780	$13,478	$13,771	$12,610
■ Federal	$3,240	$2,832	$3,043	$3,422	$3,111	$3,085	$3,090	$3,024	$2,976	$2,929	$3,456	$4,134	$4,505	$4,985	$5,254

Figure 4.7: New Brunswick Welfare Income, Single Parent, One Child (2002 dollars)

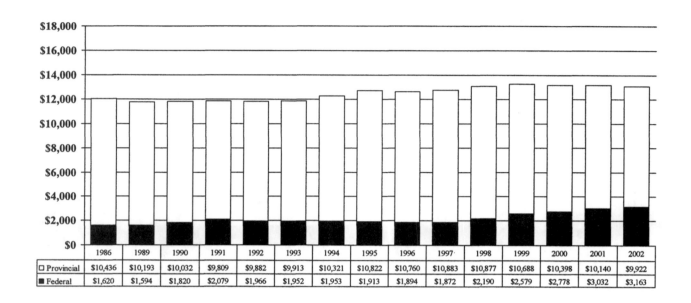

	1986	1989	1990	1991	1992	1993	1994	1995	1996	1997	1998	1999	2000	2001	2002
☐ Provincial	$10,436	$10,193	$10,032	$9,809	$9,882	$9,913	$10,321	$10,822	$10,760	$10,883	$10,877	$10,688	$10,398	$10,140	$9,922
■ Federal	$1,620	$1,594	$1,820	$2,079	$1,966	$1,952	$1,953	$1,913	$1,894	$1,872	$2,190	$2,579	$2,778	$3,032	$3,163

Figure 4.8: New Brunswick Welfare Income, Couple, Two Children (2002 dollars)

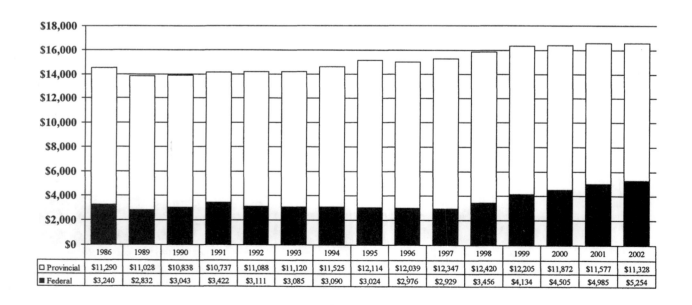

	1986	1989	1990	1991	1992	1993	1994	1995	1996	1997	1998	1999	2000	2001	2002
☐ Provincial	$11,290	$11,028	$10,838	$10,737	$11,088	$11,120	$11,525	$12,114	$12,039	$12,347	$12,420	$12,205	$11,872	$11,577	$11,328
■ Federal	$3,240	$2,832	$3,043	$3,422	$3,111	$3,085	$3,090	$3,024	$2,976	$2,929	$3,456	$4,134	$4,505	$4,985	$5,254

Figure 4.9: Quebec Welfare Income, Single Parent, One Child (2002 dollars)

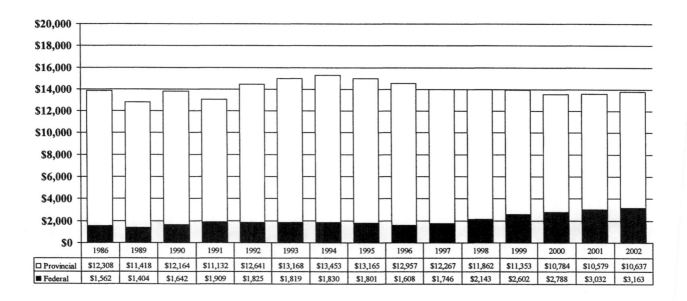

	1986	1989	1990	1991	1992	1993	1994	1995	1996	1997	1998	1999	2000	2001	2002
☐ Provincial	$12,308	$11,418	$12,164	$11,132	$12,641	$13,168	$13,453	$13,165	$12,957	$12,267	$11,862	$11,353	$10,784	$10,579	$10,637
■ Federal	$1,562	$1,404	$1,642	$1,909	$1,825	$1,819	$1,830	$1,801	$1,608	$1,746	$2,143	$2,602	$2,788	$3,032	$3,163

Figure 4.10: Quebec Welfare Income, Couple, Two Children (2002 dollars)

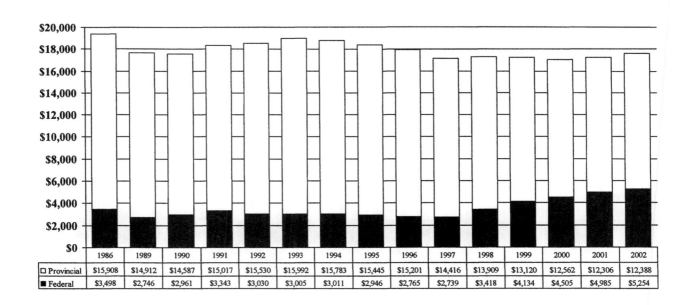

	1986	1989	1990	1991	1992	1993	1994	1995	1996	1997	1998	1999	2000	2001	2002
☐ Provincial	$15,908	$14,912	$14,587	$15,017	$15,530	$15,992	$15,783	$15,445	$15,201	$14,416	$13,909	$13,120	$12,562	$12,306	$12,388
■ Federal	$3,498	$2,746	$2,961	$3,343	$3,030	$3,005	$3,011	$2,946	$2,765	$2,739	$3,418	$4,134	$4,505	$4,985	$5,254

Figure 4.11: Ontario Welfare Income, Single Parent, One Child (2002 dollars)

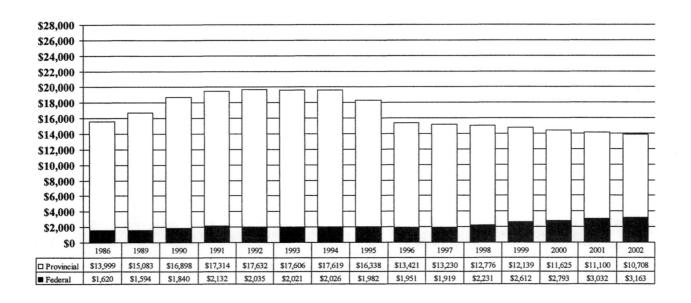

	1986	1989	1990	1991	1992	1993	1994	1995	1996	1997	1998	1999	2000	2001	2002
☐ Provincial	$13,999	$15,083	$16,898	$17,314	$17,632	$17,606	$17,619	$16,338	$13,421	$13,230	$12,776	$12,139	$11,625	$11,100	$10,708
■ Federal	$1,620	$1,594	$1,840	$2,132	$2,035	$2,021	$2,026	$1,982	$1,951	$1,919	$2,231	$2,612	$2,793	$3,032	$3,163

Figure 4.12: Ontario Welfare Income, Couple, Two Children (2002 dollars)

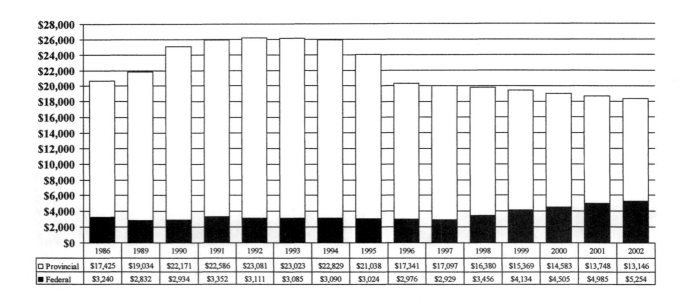

	1986	1989	1990	1991	1992	1993	1994	1995	1996	1997	1998	1999	2000	2001	2002
☐ Provincial	$17,425	$19,034	$22,171	$22,586	$23,081	$23,023	$22,829	$21,038	$17,341	$17,097	$16,380	$15,369	$14,583	$13,748	$13,146
■ Federal	$3,240	$2,832	$2,934	$3,352	$3,111	$3,085	$3,090	$3,024	$2,976	$2,929	$3,456	$4,134	$4,505	$4,985	$5,254

Figure 4.13: Manitoba Welfare Income, Single Parent, One Child (2002 dollars)

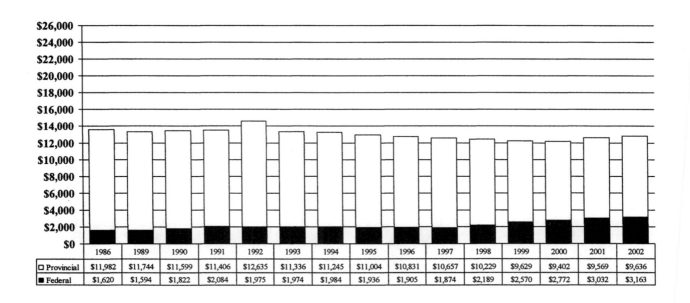

	1986	1989	1990	1991	1992	1993	1994	1995	1996	1997	1998	1999	2000	2001	2002
☐ Provincial	$11,982	$11,744	$11,599	$11,406	$12,635	$11,336	$11,245	$11,004	$10,831	$10,657	$10,229	$9,629	$9,402	$9,569	$9,636
■ Federal	$1,620	$1,594	$1,822	$2,084	$1,975	$1,974	$1,984	$1,936	$1,905	$1,874	$2,189	$2,570	$2,772	$3,032	$3,163

Figure 4.14: Manitoba Welfare Income, Couple, Two Children (2002 dollars)

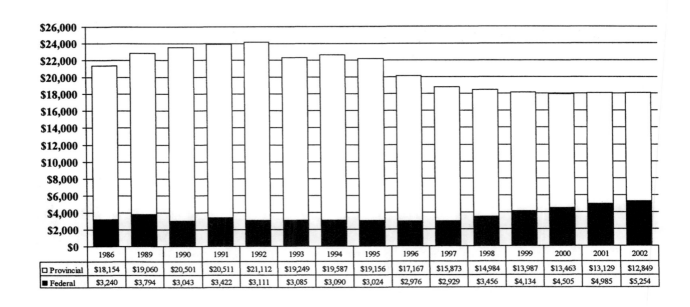

	1986	1989	1990	1991	1992	1993	1994	1995	1996	1997	1998	1999	2000	2001	2002
☐ Provincial	$18,154	$19,060	$20,501	$20,511	$21,112	$19,249	$19,587	$19,156	$17,167	$15,873	$14,984	$13,987	$13,463	$13,129	$12,849
■ Federal	$3,240	$3,794	$3,043	$3,422	$3,111	$3,085	$3,090	$3,024	$2,976	$2,929	$3,456	$4,134	$4,505	$4,985	$5,254

Figure 4.15: Saskatchewan Welfare Income, Single Parent, One Child (2002 dollars)

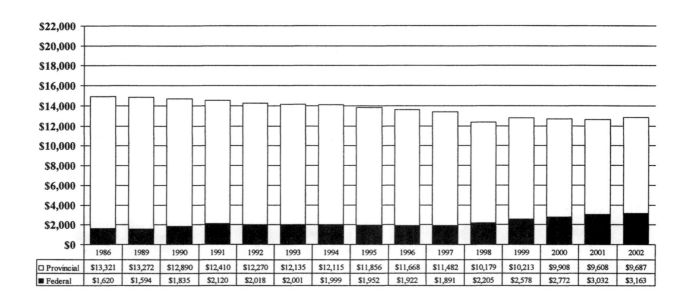

	1986	1989	1990	1991	1992	1993	1994	1995	1996	1997	1998	1999	2000	2001	2002
□ Provincial	$13,321	$13,272	$12,890	$12,410	$12,270	$12,135	$12,115	$11,856	$11,668	$11,482	$10,179	$10,213	$9,908	$9,608	$9,687
■ Federal	$1,620	$1,594	$1,835	$2,120	$2,018	$2,001	$1,999	$1,952	$1,922	$1,891	$2,205	$2,578	$2,772	$3,032	$3,163

Figure 4.16: Saskatchewan Welfare Income, Couple, Two Children (2002 dollars)

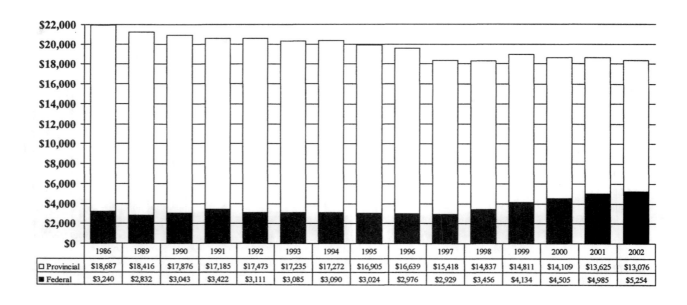

	1986	1989	1990	1991	1992	1993	1994	1995	1996	1997	1998	1999	2000	2001	2002
□ Provincial	$18,687	$18,416	$17,876	$17,185	$17,473	$17,235	$17,272	$16,905	$16,639	$15,418	$14,837	$14,811	$14,109	$13,625	$13,076
■ Federal	$3,240	$2,832	$3,043	$3,422	$3,111	$3,085	$3,090	$3,024	$2,976	$2,929	$3,456	$4,134	$4,505	$4,985	$5,254

Figure 4.17: Alberta Welfare Income, Single Parent, One Child (2002 dollars)

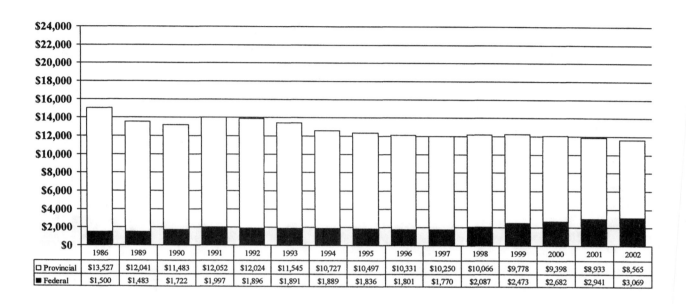

	1986	1989	1990	1991	1992	1993	1994	1995	1996	1997	1998	1999	2000	2001	2002
☐ Provincial	$13,527	$12,041	$11,483	$12,052	$12,024	$11,545	$10,727	$10,497	$10,331	$10,250	$10,066	$9,778	$9,398	$8,933	$8,565
■ Federal	$1,500	$1,483	$1,722	$1,997	$1,896	$1,891	$1,889	$1,836	$1,801	$1,770	$2,087	$2,473	$2,682	$2,941	$3,069

Figure 4.18: Alberta Welfare Income, Couple, Two Children (2002 dollars)

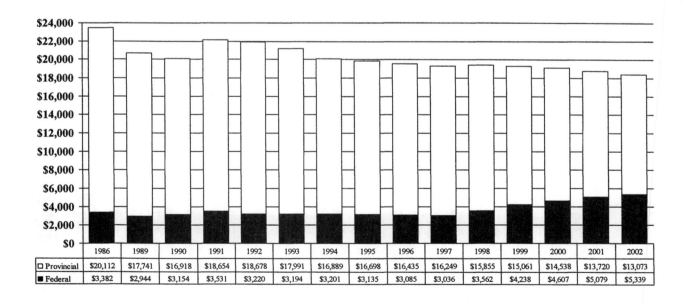

	1986	1989	1990	1991	1992	1993	1994	1995	1996	1997	1998	1999	2000	2001	2002
☐ Provincial	$20,112	$17,741	$16,918	$18,654	$18,678	$17,991	$16,889	$16,698	$16,435	$16,249	$15,855	$15,061	$14,538	$13,720	$13,073
■ Federal	$3,382	$2,944	$3,154	$3,531	$3,220	$3,194	$3,201	$3,135	$3,085	$3,036	$3,562	$4,238	$4,607	$5,079	$5,339

Figure 4.19: British Columbia Welfare Income, Single Parent, One Child (2002 dollars)

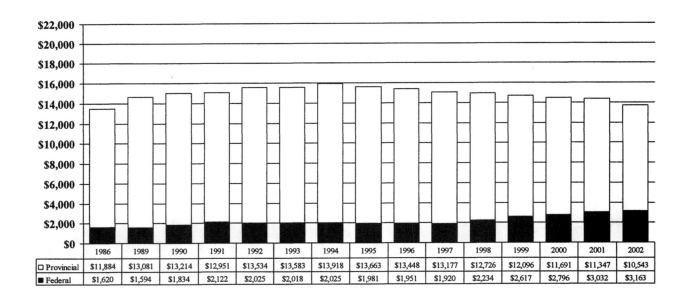

	1986	1989	1990	1991	1992	1993	1994	1995	1996	1997	1998	1999	2000	2001	2002
□ Provincial	$11,884	$13,081	$13,214	$12,951	$13,534	$13,583	$13,918	$13,663	$13,448	$13,177	$12,726	$12,096	$11,691	$11,347	$10,543
■ Federal	$1,620	$1,594	$1,834	$2,122	$2,025	$2,018	$2,025	$1,981	$1,951	$1,920	$2,234	$2,617	$2,796	$3,032	$3,163

Figure 4.20: British Columbia Welfare Income, Couple, Two Children (2002 dollars)

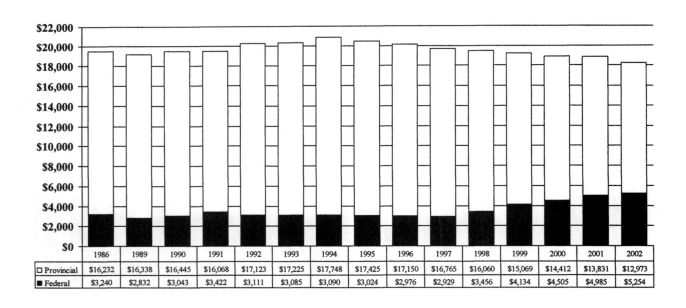

	1986	1989	1990	1991	1992	1993	1994	1995	1996	1997	1998	1999	2000	2001	2002
□ Provincial	$16,232	$16,338	$16,445	$16,068	$17,123	$17,225	$17,748	$17,425	$17,150	$16,765	$16,060	$15,069	$14,412	$13,831	$12,973
■ Federal	$3,240	$2,832	$3,043	$3,422	$3,111	$3,085	$3,090	$3,024	$2,976	$2,929	$3,456	$4,134	$4,505	$4,985	$5,254

Figure 4.21: Yukon Welfare Income, Single Parent, One Child (2002 dollars)

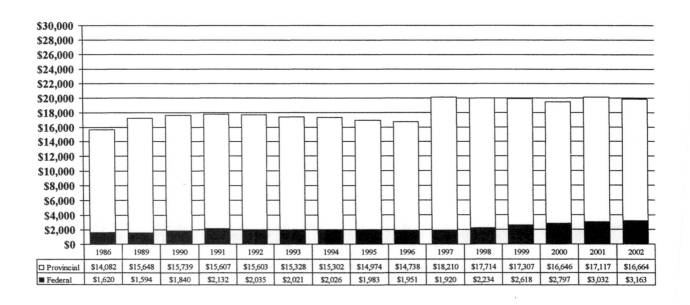

	1986	1989	1990	1991	1992	1993	1994	1995	1996	1997	1998	1999	2000	2001	2002
□ Provincial	$14,082	$15,648	$15,739	$15,607	$15,603	$15,328	$15,302	$14,974	$14,738	$18,210	$17,714	$17,307	$16,646	$17,117	$16,664
■ Federal	$1,620	$1,594	$1,840	$2,132	$2,035	$2,021	$2,026	$1,983	$1,951	$1,920	$2,234	$2,618	$2,797	$3,032	$3,163

Figure 4.22: Yukon Welfare Income, Couple, Two Children (2002 dollars)

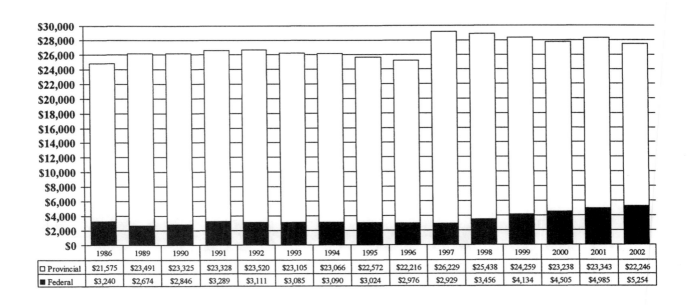

	1986	1989	1990	1991	1992	1993	1994	1995	1996	1997	1998	1999	2000	2001	2002
□ Provincial	$21,575	$23,491	$23,325	$23,328	$23,520	$23,105	$23,066	$22,572	$22,216	$26,229	$25,438	$24,259	$23,238	$23,343	$22,246
■ Federal	$3,240	$2,674	$2,846	$3,289	$3,111	$3,085	$3,090	$3,024	$2,976	$2,929	$3,456	$4,134	$4,505	$4,985	$5,254

Figure 4.23: Northwest Territories Welfare Income, Single Parent, One Child (2002 dollars)

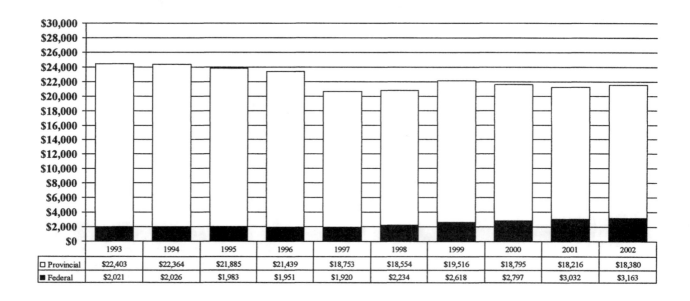

	1993	1994	1995	1996	1997	1998	1999	2000	2001	2002
☐ Provincial	$22,403	$22,364	$21,885	$21,439	$18,753	$18,554	$19,516	$18,795	$18,216	$18,380
■ Federal	$2,021	$2,026	$1,983	$1,951	$1,920	$2,234	$2,618	$2,797	$3,032	$3,163

Figure 4.24: Northwest Territories Welfare Income, Couple, Two Children (2002 dollars)

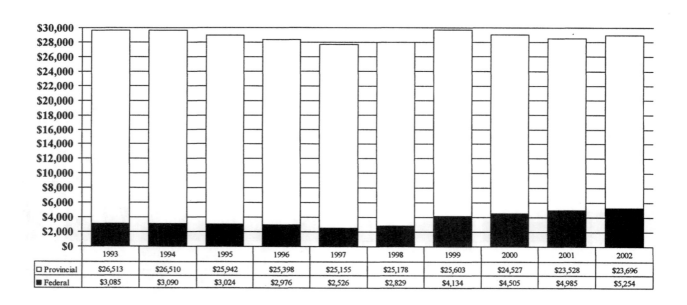

	1993	1994	1995	1996	1997	1998	1999	2000	2001	2002
☐ Provincial	$26,513	$26,510	$25,942	$25,398	$25,155	$25,178	$25,603	$24,527	$23,528	$23,696
■ Federal	$3,085	$3,090	$3,024	$2,976	$2,526	$2,829	$4,134	$4,505	$4,985	$5,254

Figure 4.25: Nunavut Welfare Income, Single Parent, One Child (2002 dollars)

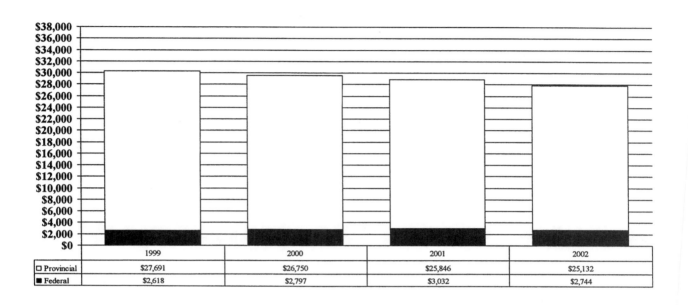

	1999	2000	2001	2002
□ Provincial	$27,691	$26,750	$25,846	$25,132
■ Federal	$2,618	$2,797	$3,032	$2,744

Figure 4.26: Nunavut Welfare Income, Couple, Two Children (2002 dollars)

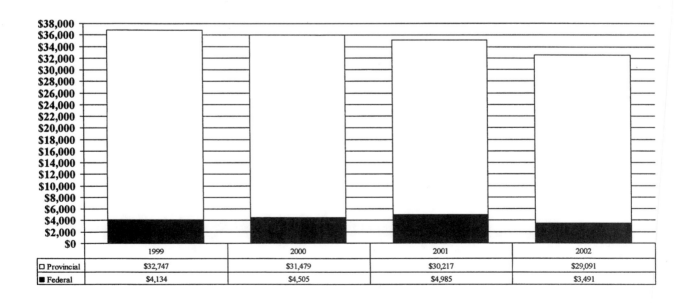

	1999	2000	2001	2002
□ Provincial	$32,747	$31,479	$30,217	$29,091
■ Federal	$4,134	$4,505	$4,985	$3,491

V. WELFARE INCOMES AND POVERTY OVER TIME

In the years in which the National Council of Welfare has examined welfare rates, provincial and territorial governments have frequently made changes to their welfare programs. Table 5.1 examines the impact these changes had on the adequacy of welfare incomes in the period from 1986 to 2002. We have included the total income of welfare recipients, including basic social assistance from provincial and territorial governments, federal, provincial and territorial child benefits, GST credits and provincial tax credits. For each year, the incomes are shown as a percentage of the poverty line. This calculation ensures that the comparisons take into consideration factors such as the size of families and communities. This also allows us to make comparisons across provinces.

The territories are not included in this table because they are excluded from the Statistics Canada survey that is used to generate the low income cut-offs. The National Council of Welfare did not include a single person with a disability in its original calculations of welfare incomes for 1986, so the figures for people with disabilities begin in 1989.

The last column of Table 5.1 shows that between 2001 and 2002, the standard of living for people on welfare declined for most cases. Incomes dropped for all household types in Ontario, Alberta, and British Colombia. In Nova Scotia, the single parent and the couple with children saw the adequacy of their welfare income drop by 1.2 percent and five percent respectively. Single employable people and single people with disabilities in Newfoundland, Prince Edward Island, New Brunswick, Manitoba, and Saskatchewan also lost more ground in 2002. In Newfoundland and New Brunswick, the single parent with one child fell behind. In Manitoba and Saskatchewan, couples with two children also fell behind.

Only the couples with two children in Newfoundland and Labrador, Prince Edward Island, and New Brunswick saw a 0.2, 1.3 and 0.1 percent improvement respectively in the adequacy of their welfare incomes in 2002. In Manitoba and Saskatchewan, only the single parents with one child saw a 1.5 percent and a 1.6 percent improvement.

Quebec was the only province than showed gains in the standard of living for all family types in 2002.

The column showing changes between 1986 and 2002 shows that the majority of household types realized losses in their standard of living over this sixteen-year period. The largest gains were made by the single employable person in Quebec. The greatest losses were those of the single employable person in Alberta whose income was 51 percent of the poverty line in 1986 but was only 26 percent of the poverty line by 2002.

At no point between 1986 and 2002 did any province or territory provide welfare benefits that allowed welfare recipients to reach the poverty line. As Table 5.1 shows, the highest rates ever achieved were still substantially below the poverty line and have since deteriorated significantly.

Between 1989 and 2002, single employable people in Prince Edward Island lost the most ground in their standard of living. Their incomes were worth 66 percent of the poverty line in 1989, and only 36 percent by 2002. This represents a drop of 81.4 percent.

The poorest of all welfare recipients in Canada are always single employable people. Newfoundland shares with New Brunswick the distinction of providing the lowest welfare income to single employable people at only 20 percent of the poverty line in 2002.

Since 1989, the welfare incomes of people with disabilities have steadily eroded. In every province except Quebec and Manitoba, these welfare incomes are a much lower percentage of the poverty line in 2002 than they were in 1989. Although there were minor gains made in some intervening years in some provinces, every gain has been lost over time.

Between 1986 and 2002, single parent families with one child lost ground in most provinces with the exception of Newfoundland, New Brunswick, Quebec and British Colombia. In Alberta, the welfare income of the single-parent family was at an all-time low of 48 percent of the poverty line in 2002, the lowest standard of living for a single parent in the country. The highest percentage for this household type was in Newfoundland at 72 percent of the poverty line in 2002 which is down from 73 percent in 2001.

A couple with two children ages 10 and 15 in Quebec experienced the lowest standard of living in Canada at only 49 percent of the poverty line in 2002. This was a major drop from 54 percent in 1989. The couple with two children in New Brunswick experienced the biggest gains in this time period. The highest percentage for this household type was in Prince Edward Island at 65 percent of the poverty line in 2002 down from a high of 78 percent in 1989.

Welfare incomes in all the provinces are grossly inadequate and in most cases are far less adequate than they were in 1989. The National Council of Welfare is extremely concerned about this trend. The poorest of the poor are falling farther behind and the gap between the haves and have nots widens in a country often regarded as the best place live in the world.

On the next pages, Figures 5.1 and 5.2 illustrate that single employable people are consistently the most impoverished groups on welfare in all the provinces. Figures 5.3 and 5.4 show that single people with disabilities live at a poverty level only slightly better. For both groups of people on welfare, already low welfare benefits have in general eroded slowly over time.

TABLE 5.1: 2002 WELFARE INCOME AS PERCENTAGE OF THE POVERTY LINE

	1986	1989	1990	1991	1992	1993	1994	1995	1996	1997	1998	1999	2000	2001	2002	% Change 1986-2002	% Change 1989-2002	% Change 2001-2002
NEWFOUNDLAND AND LABRADOR																		
Single Employable	33	32	32	33	34	33	33	33	19	9	9	9	12	20	20	-63.1%	-60.2%	-1.5%
Person with a Disability		64	63	63	64	63	63	62	61	60	60	59	56	55	54		-18.4%	-1.9%
Single Parent, One Child	68	66	67	69	71	71	70	69	68	67	69	70	72	73	72	6.1%	8.6%	-0.6%
Couple, Two Children	58	56	56	56	56	55	55	54	53	53	54	56	57	57	58	-0.6%	2.7%	0.2%
PRINCE EDWARD ISLAND																		
Single Employable	62	66	60	62	62	62	56	43	40	39	39	38	37	36	36	-70.2%	-81.4%	-0.1%
Person with a Disability		77	70	70	71	70	69	67	67	60	60	59	56	55	55		-41.0%	-0.1%
Single Parent, One Child	71	75	69	71	71	71	70	67	64	62	61	60	63	62	63	-11.7%	-18.5%	1.3%
Couple, Two Children	74	78	71	73	73	73	71	69	64	64	63	62	64	64	65	-13.1%	-19.9%	1.3%
NOVA SCOTIA																		
Single Employable	44	50	48	47	46	45	45	44	43	32	32	31	29	30	31	-41.5%	-59.1%	5.1%
Person with a Disability		66	66	66	65	64	65	63	62	61	61	60	56	51	53		-23.6%	3.7%
Single Parent, One Child	64	66	66	67	67	66	67	65	64	63	63	63	64	61	60	-7.4%	-10.2%	-1.2%
Couple, Two Children	57	60	58	58	57	56	56	55	58	59	59	57	58	60	57	0.8%	-4.4%	-5.0%
NEW BRUNSWICK																		
Single Employable	22	24	24	25	24	24	24	24	24	23	23	23	21	21	20	-7.1%	-17.3%	-2.1%
Person with a Disability		63	62	62	61	61	61	48	47	48	48	47	44	43	42		-50.7%	-2.1%
Single Parent, One Child	56	55	55	55	55	55	57	59	59	59	61	62	64	64	63	11.5%	13.2%	-0.7%
Couple, Two Children	46	44	44	45	45	45	46	48	48	49	50	52	53	53	53	13.4%	17.5%	0.1%
QUEBEC																		
Single Employable	20	31	48	41	41	41	40	39	39	37	37	37	34	34	35	41.4%	10.3%	1.5%
Person with a Disability		47	49	53	53	53	54	53	53	53	53	53	49	49	50		5.4%	0.5%
Single Parent, One Child	57	54	58	54	59	60	62	61	60	57	57	57	56	57	57	1.2%	5.8%	1.4%
Couple, Two Children	54	54	59	52	52	53	52	51	51	48	48	48	47	48	49	-11.3%	-10.9%	2.0%

TABLE 5.1: 2002 WELFARE INCOME AS PERCENTAGE OF THE POVERTY LINE

	1986	1989	1990	1991	1992	1993	1994	1995	1996	1997	1998	1999	2000	2001	2002	% Change 1986-2002	% Change 1989-2002	% Change 2001-2002
ONTARIO																		
Single Employable	43	47	52	54	55	55	55	51	42	42	41	41	37	36	35	-22.0%	-32.4%	-2.1%
Person with a Disability		68	72	75	76	76	76	74	73	72	71	70	64	62	61		-11.3%	-2.2%
Single Parent, One Child	64	68	76	79	80	80	80	75	63	62	61	60	60	59	58	-10.7%	-18.0%	-1.9%
Couple, Two Children	58	61	70	72	73	73	72	67	57	56	55	55	53	52	51	-13.6%	-20.1%	-1.8%
MANITOBA																		
Single Employable	43	40	46	46	47	47	44	42	39	34	34	33	30	29	29	-48.7%	-38.5%	-2.1%
Person with a Disability		43	49	49	59	53	53	52	51	50	50	49	45	44	43		0.9%	-2.2%
Single Parent, One Child	56	50	54	55	60	54	54	53	52	51	51	50	51	52	53	-4.5%	6.0%	1.5%
Couple, Two Children	60	60	65	67	68	63	64	62	56	52	51	50	50	50	50	-19.6%	-20.1%	-0.1%
SASKATCHEWAN																		
Single Employable	41	42	41	41	42	44	44	43	42	38	38	39	37	37	36	-12.4%	-15.3%	-1.5%
Person with a Disability		67	65	65	63	63	63	61	62	56	56	57	54	54	53		-27.5%	-2.0%
Single Parent, One Child	70	69	68	68	66	66	66	64	63	62	58	59	61	61	62	-11.7%	-10.9%	1.6%
Couple, Two Children	70	68	66	65	65	65	65	63	62	58	58	60	60	60	59	-18.2%	-15.3%	-1.5%
ALBERTA																		
Single Employable	51	36	35	39	38	36	32	31	31	30	30	30	27	27	26	-95.7%	-37.7%	-2.1%
Person with a Disability		44	43	60	45	44	44	43	42	42	42	42	41	40	39		-11.5%	-2.1%
Single Parent, One Child	61	55	53	57	57	54	52	50	50	49	50	50	50	49	48	-27.0%	-13.8%	-2.1%
Couple, Two Children	66	58	56	62	61	59	56	55	55	54	54	54	53	52	51	-29.1%	-14.1%	-2.1%
BRITISH COLUMBIA																		
Single Employable	37	41	42	40	43	43	44	43	39	39	38	38	35	34	34	-8.9%	-22.2%	-2.1%
Person with a Disability		56	58	58	60	60	61	61	60	59	58	57	53	52	51		-10.2%	-2.2%
Single Parent, One Child	55	60	61	62	64	64	65	64	63	62	61	60	60	60	57	3.1%	-5.4%	-4.9%
Couple, Two Children	54	53	54	54	56	57	57	57	56	55	54	54	52	52	50	-8.1%	-5.4%	-3.2%

The adequacy of welfare incomes has declined, but there is a variation in that pattern, even within regions. Among the five eastern provinces shown in Figure 5.1, the most consistently low incomes for single employable people were in New Brunswick. In 1986, the New Brunswick income for a single employable person was worth only 22 percent of the poverty line, and this has barely fluctuated since. By 2002, the New Brunswick income was 20 percent. In Newfoundland, the single employable person had an income worth 33 percent of the poverty line in 1986. In 1996, the provincial government imposed a severe cut to the welfare rates of single employable people, bringing their incomes down to only nine percent of the poverty line. In 2000, Newfoundland relented on this draconian practice. A single employable person in Newfoundland received all of 20 percent of the poverty line in 2002 – tied with New Brunswick and still the least adequate welfare rate in the country.

The least inadequate welfare income in Canada for a single employable person was 66 percent of the poverty line in Prince Edward Island in 1989. By 2002, this rate had deteriorated to 36 percent of the poverty line, the worst income PEI had ever provided to single employable people who are down on their luck.

In the five western provinces shown in Figure 5.2 there were also significant changes in the value of welfare incomes for single employable people. The value of Manitoba's welfare dropped from 43 percent in 1986 to only 29 percent by 2002. In Saskatchewan, the value of welfare dropped from 41 percent of the poverty line to 36 percent in 2002. In British Columbia, welfare was worth 37 percent of the poverty line in 1986, climbed to 44 percent by 1994, and had dropped to only 34 percent by 2002.

The most striking changes were in Alberta and in Ontario. In Alberta, the value of welfare dropped from 51 percent of the poverty line in 1986 to an all-time low of 26 percent by 2002. In Ontario, the value of welfare for a single employable person was only 43 percent of the poverty line in 1986, but rose to 55 percent for 1992 and 1993. By 2002, the single person on welfare in Ontario subsisted on only 35 percent of the poverty line.

The 2002 welfare incomes for people with disabilities have declined in value in the years the National Council of Welfare has tracked the situation. Welfare rates for people with disabilities are consistently better than those for people considered employable, but they are still very low. While this group of welfare recipients was often spared the direct cuts to welfare, their incomes were not spared from the erosion of inflation and freezes to increases in benefits.

Figure 5.3 shows the slow and steady decline in value in Newfoundland from 64 percent of the poverty line in 1989 to 54 percent by 2002. In PEI, a single person with a disability had an income worth 77 percent of the poverty line in 1989 – the highest in the country at the time. By 2002, it was worth only 54 percent. In Nova Scotia, the income was worth 66 percent of the poverty line in 1989, then declined in value slowly until it was worth 53 percent of the poverty line in 2002. A disabled person in Quebec had an income worth only 47 percent of the poverty line in 1989. That income increased in value to 54 percent in 1994, then declined to 50 percent by 2002. New Brunswick's welfare for a single disabled person was worth 63 percent of the poverty line in 1989, then dropped significantly in 1995 to 48 percent of the poverty line, and has declined since to only 42 percent of the poverty line.

Figure 5.4 shows the adequacy of welfare for single disabled people in the five western provinces. The value of the welfare for a single disabled person in Ontario rose in value from 68 percent in 1989 to 76 percent from 1992 to 1994. Although disabled people were spared the drastic cuts Ontario imposed on all other people on welfare in 1994, their incomes deteriorated slowly, reaching 61 percent of the poverty line by 2002. Manitoba's welfare for a single disabled person was worth 43 percent of the poverty line in 1989, and then rose slowly to reach 59 percent of the poverty line by 1992. It has since deteriorated and is now worth 43 percent of the poverty line. Saskatchewan's income was worth 67 percent of the poverty line in 1989, but has deteriorated steadily throughout this period to 53 percent of the poverty line in 2002.

Alberta gave assistance worth 44 percent of the poverty line in 1989, which rose to 60 percent of the line in 1991, and has deteriorated since then to 39 percent. It should be noted that most people with severe and permanent disabilities in Alberta qualified for the Assured Income for the Severely Handicapped program which provided a higher rate.

In British Columbia, a single disabled person had an income worth 56 percent of the poverty line in 1989, which rose to 61 percent of the poverty line in 1994 and 1995, and has since declined to 51 percent of the poverty line.

Figure 5.1: Welfare Incomes over Time as % of Poverty Line, Single Employable People

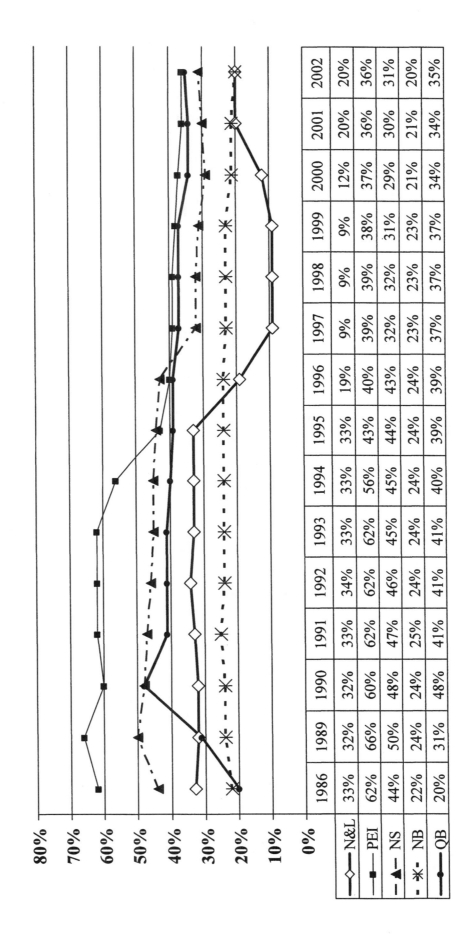

	1986	1989	1990	1991	1992	1993	1994	1995	1996	1997	1998	1999	2000	2001	2002
N&L	33%	32%	32%	33%	34%	33%	33%	33%	19%	9%	9%	9%	12%	20%	20%
PEI	62%	66%	60%	62%	62%	62%	56%	43%	40%	39%	39%	38%	37%	36%	36%
NS	44%	50%	48%	47%	46%	45%	45%	44%	43%	32%	32%	31%	29%	30%	31%
NB	22%	24%	24%	25%	24%	24%	24%	24%	24%	23%	23%	23%	21%	21%	20%
QB	20%	31%	48%	41%	41%	41%	40%	39%	39%	37%	37%	37%	34%	34%	35%

Figure 5.2: Welfare Incomes over Time as % of Poverty Line, Single Employable People

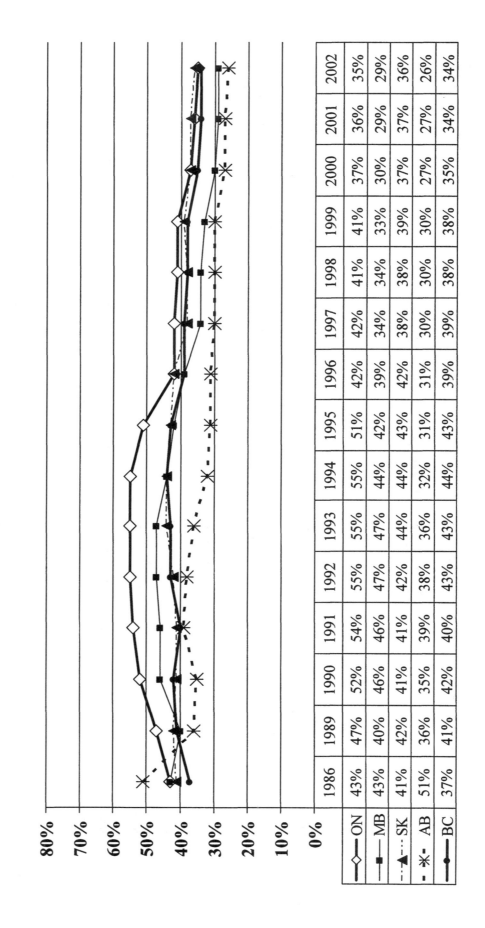

	1986	1989	1990	1991	1992	1993	1994	1995	1996	1997	1998	1999	2000	2001	2002
ON	43%	47%	52%	54%	55%	55%	55%	51%	42%	42%	41%	41%	37%	36%	35%
MB	43%	40%	46%	46%	47%	47%	44%	42%	39%	34%	34%	33%	30%	29%	29%
SK	41%	42%	41%	41%	42%	44%	44%	43%	42%	38%	38%	39%	37%	37%	36%
AB	51%	36%	35%	39%	38%	36%	32%	31%	31%	30%	30%	30%	27%	27%	26%
BC	37%	41%	42%	40%	43%	43%	44%	43%	39%	39%	38%	38%	35%	34%	34%

NATIONAL COUNCIL OF WELFARE

Figure 5.3: Welfare Incomes over Time as % of Poverty Line, Person with a Disability

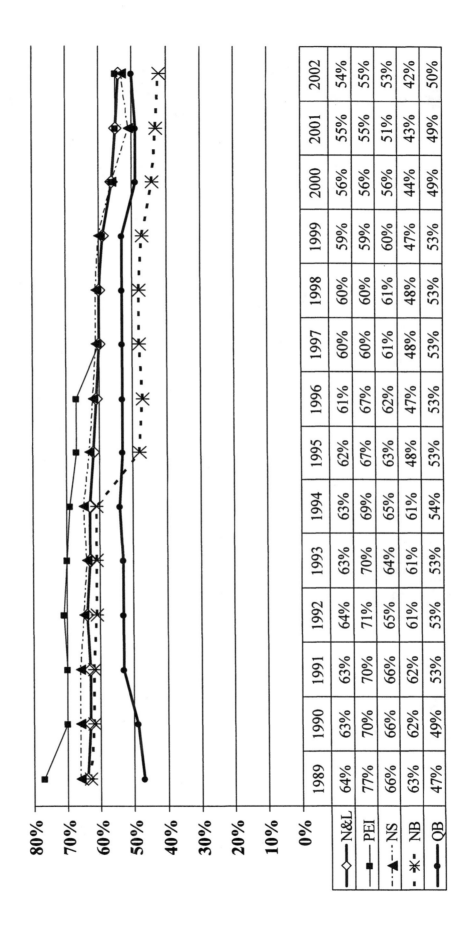

	1989	1990	1991	1992	1993	1994	1995	1996	1997	1998	1999	2000	2001	2002
N&L	64%	63%	63%	64%	63%	63%	62%	61%	60%	60%	59%	56%	55%	54%
PEI	77%	70%	70%	71%	70%	69%	67%	67%	60%	60%	59%	56%	55%	55%
NS	66%	66%	66%	65%	64%	65%	63%	62%	61%	61%	60%	56%	51%	53%
NB	63%	62%	62%	61%	61%	61%	48%	47%	48%	48%	47%	44%	43%	42%
QB	47%	49%	53%	53%	53%	54%	53%	53%	53%	53%	53%	49%	49%	50%

Figure 5.4: Welfare Incomes over Time as % of Poverty Line, Person with a Disability

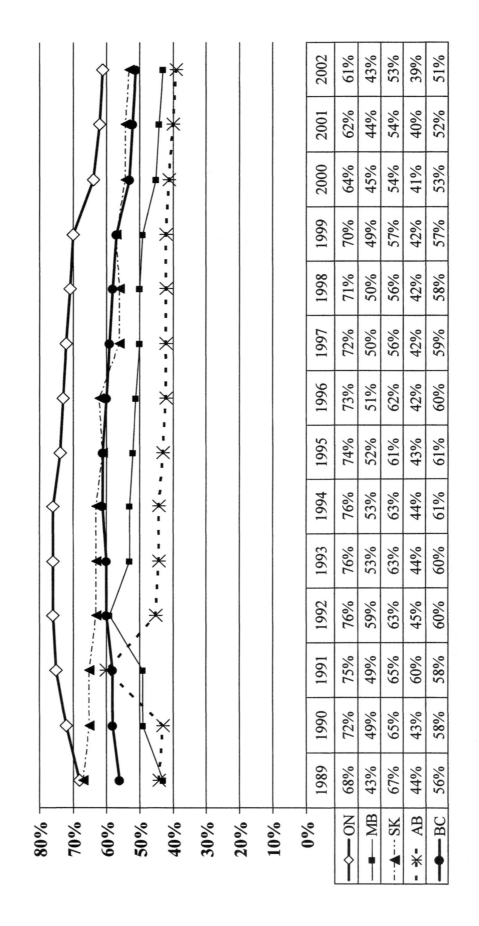

	1989	1990	1991	1992	1993	1994	1995	1996	1997	1998	1999	2000	2001	2002
ON	68%	72%	75%	76%	76%	76%	74%	73%	72%	71%	70%	64%	62%	61%
MB	43%	49%	49%	59%	53%	53%	52%	51%	50%	50%	49%	45%	44%	43%
SK	67%	65%	65%	63%	63%	63%	61%	62%	56%	56%	57%	54%	54%	53%
AB	44%	43%	60%	45%	44%	44%	43%	42%	42%	42%	42%	41%	40%	39%
BC	56%	58%	58%	60%	60%	61%	61%	60%	59%	58%	57%	53%	52%	51%

VI. EARNINGS EXEMPTIONS

The figures in the tables in this report do not take into account the fact that welfare incomes may be higher if recipients have additional earnings. Each province and territory allows welfare recipients to retain a certain amount of earned income (a flat-rate sum, a percentage of earnings or a combination of both) without any reduction in their welfare cheques. The National Council of Welfare did not include these extra amounts in the tables in this report because it is not certain that recipients could actually increase their incomes by these levels. They may be unable to work or unable to find jobs.

Table 6.1 shows the allowable earnings exemptions for January 2002 in each province and territory. The exemptions vary by family size and sometimes by employability. All provinces and territories recognize work-related expenses, including childcare expenses in most cases. Welfare recipients are allowed to deduct all or some of these costs when declaring their earnings for welfare purposes. In effect, that means that the actual earnings exemptions in some provinces and territories may be more generous than they appear at first glance. Earnings exemptions also provide a greater incentive for people to take paying jobs.

Earnings exemptions are important because they provide a means for welfare recipients to improve the quality of their lives, at least marginally. These exemptions encourage individuals to get experience in the labour market and to gain sufficient confidence to leave the welfare system.

No one would disagree that sensible earnings exemption policies offer genuine incentives for people on welfare to improve their financial situation by taking a job. But earnings exemptions, no matter how generous, are no substitute for adequate welfare rates. Paying decent welfare rates and improving incentives to work by increasing earnings exemptions is sound social policy. Cutting benefits or earnings exemptions is not.

In 2002, several provinces reduced or eliminated the monthly earnings exemptions for families on welfare as well as for single employable people. British Columbia eliminated all monthly earnings exemptions for employable single people and for families effective April 1, 2002. These changes will be reflected in next year's *Welfare Incomes*. Nova Scotia eliminated the flat-rate earnings exemptions and replaced it with a percentage of earnings only for everyone except the disabled single person. Saskatchewan introduced a ceiling of $375 for singles and $625 for families to the exemption of 20 percent of earnings.

Northwest Territories and Nunavut increased the flat-rate monthly earnings exemption by $50 for singles and $100 for families. Yukon increased the flat-rate monthly earnings exemption by $50 for all family types. Manitoba introduced a 30 percent monthly earnings exemption for the single unemployable person. New Brunswick introduced a variable percentage of monthly earnings exemption that is higher for the first six months and then drops for another six months ending with a flat rate exemption only.

TABLE 6.1: MONTHLY EARNINGS EXEMPTIONS AS OF JANUARY 2002

	Unemployable	Employable
NEWFOUNDLAND AND LABRADOR[1]	Disabled adult: up to $95 Family with disabled member(s): up to $190	Unemployed adult: up to $75 Family of two or more (no disabled members): up to $150
PRINCE EDWARD ISLAND[2]	$50 for a single adult or $100 for a family plus 10% of the balance of net wages for both households	
NOVA SCOTIA[3]	Single adult or family: 30% of net earnings or vocational training allowances Single disabled adult in an approved education program: $150 + 30% of monthly training allowances	Single adult or family: 30% of net wages
NEW BRUNSWICK	Single adult: $150 to $200[4] Family: $200 to $250[4]	Welfare recipients are eligible for the Extended Wage Exemption when their earnings are high enough that the application of the extended wage exemption is to their benefit, and where the employment seems likely to lead to self-sufficiency (that is, is not temporary or seasonal). The Extended Wage Exemption lasts for 12 months only. Recipients' exemptions then revert to the established exemption minimum. Single person and couple without children: 30% of net earned income for the first six months, 25% of net earned income for the next six months, then flat exemption of $150 or $200 a month. Family with children: 35% of net earned income for the first six months, 30% of net earned income for the next six months, then flat exemption of $200 a month.

TABLE 6.1: MONTHLY EARNINGS EXEMPTIONS AS OF JANUARY 2002

	Unemployable	Employable
QUEBEC	Adult with severe limitation to work: $100 Adult with temporary limitation to work: $200	Single adult: $200 Single parent: $200 Two-parent family: $300
ONTARIO	Disabled single adult: $160 + 25% of remainder of earnings + disability related expenses for a maximum of $140 Disabled adult with family: $235 + 25% of remainder of earnings + disability related expenses for a maximum of $140 + child care[5]	Single adult: first $143 + variable exemption[6] Single parent, one child: first $275 + variable exemption + child care[7] Couple, two children: first $346 + variable exemption + child care
MANITOBA[8]	Single adult and for a spouse: $100 month + 30% of net monthly earnings over $100 Single disabled parent: $115 month + 30% of net earnings over $115	Single adult, childless couple and two-parent family with children: $100 for each earner + 25% of net earnings over $100 Single parent: $115 + 25% of net earnings over $115
SASKATCHEWAN[9]	Single disabled adult: first $100 of earned income + 20% of next $375 (maximum exemption $175) Two-adult family, no children: first $125 of earned income + 20% of next $625 (maximum exemption $250) Family with children in which the adult is disabled: $200. Earnings over $200 are eligible for the Saskatchewan Employment Supplement.[10]	Single person: first $25 of earned income + 20% of next $375 (maximum exemption $100) Two-adult family, no children: first $50 of earned income + 20% of next $625 (maximum exemption of $175) Family with children: $125. Earnings over $125 are eligible for the Saskatchewan Employment Supplement.

TABLE 6.1: MONTHLY EARNINGS EXEMPTIONS AS OF JANUARY 2002

	Unemployable	Employable
ALBERTA	Each adult worker in family: $115 plus 25% of net income earned by all adults. First $350 of earnings of each child in the family plus 25% of income over $350 earned by the children.[11]	
BRITISH COLUMBIA	Disability Benefits Level 1 (temporarily unemployable): eligible for the regular earnings exemption. Disability Benefits Level 2 (permanently unemployable): $200 + 25% of remaining amount. There is no time limit.[12]	Single adult: $100 + 25% of any income earned after recipient has been on welfare for three months.[13] Couple and families: $200 + 25% of any income earned after recipient has been on welfare for three months.[14] The exemption is available for only twelve months during a 36-month period. The twelve months need not be consecutive.
YUKON	For first three months on welfare, $50 for a single adult, $100 for a family. In fourth month, an additional exemption of 25% of net income. No exemption on net income from full-time employment (more than 20 hours a week). Earnings exemption on part-time employment is the greater of 50% of net earnings (not exceeding 25% of the total of items of basic requirements necessary to maintain an applicant and dependants) or $5 a month for a single person, $10 a month for a couple and $15 a month for a family of three or more. People considered to be permanently excluded: $25 for a single adult; $50 for a married couple from sale of handicrafts or hobby materials.	
NORTHWEST TERRITORIES[15]	$200 (no dependants) $400 (dependants)	
NUNAVUT[16]	$150 (no dependants) $300 (dependants)	

Newfoundland and Labrador

[1] In October 1998, Newfoundland and Labrador increased the deduction from earnings for private child care or the parental contribution costs for licensed day care from $200 per month to a maximum of $325 per month for one child and an additional $125 for each additional child if necessary for employment. Disabled adults or disabled members of a family must be people who require supportive services to qualify for the higher earnings exemption. In addition, the disabled member in a family can also include a disabled child if the child requires supportive services.

Prince Edward Island

[2] The earnings exemptions for welfare recipients also apply to applicants for welfare. A maximum of $25 a week may be deducted from net income where applicants or beneficiaries must travel to and from work.

Nova Scotia

[3] There is a total exemption of earned income for the first month of full-time employment for unemployable recipients. Training allowances for full-time participants are also exempt during the first month. The Director may include as a budgetary requirement up to $200 a month for child care, transportation and special clothing if needed for participation in an approved employment, education or rehabilitation program. In 2001, flat rate deductibles were eliminated for all categories and the percentage of net earnings exemption was increased from 25 percent to 30 percent.

New Brunswick

[4] Families and individuals who are able to achieve self-reliance in a short period of time are eligible for higher wage exemption levels.

Ontario

[5] Actual amount paid for licensed child care expenses, otherwise, a maximum of $390 for children five years of age and under, $346 for children between six and 12 years of age, or $390 for children six or older who have special needs.

[6] Ontario deducts a monthly flat rate amount from net earnings. This amount varies according to family size. After the basic exemption is deducted, Ontario allows welfare recipients to keep an additional percentage of net earnings. The variable exemption decreases proportionately with the cumulative number of months the household has declared earnings. For the first 12 months, the variable exemption is 25 percent; for 13 to 24 months, it is 15 percent, and after 24 months there is no further exemption.

[7] Actual amount paid for licensed child care expenses, otherwise, a maximum of $390 for each child under 13.

Manitoba

[8] Participants are eligible for the additional percentage noted in each case after the first month on welfare. When a recipient's gross monthly income from all sources (less child care expenses) represents 135 percent or more of the household's cost of basic necessities, the recipient is no longer eligible for welfare.

Saskatchewan

[9] The earnings exemptions apply to fully employable individuals only after they have been on welfare for at least the preceding three consecutive months. Recipients in the "disabled" or "not fully employable" categories are entitled to the earnings exemption from the time they receive income from employment.

[10] The Saskatchewan Employment Supplement is a monthly payment for parents on welfare who work for pay or receive child or spousal support. The supplement is paid at a rate of 25 to 45 percent of income depending on the size of the family to a maximum of $333 extra a month for a family with five or more children. In May 2001, a supplementary benefit for children under age 13 was introduced. This supplement ranges from an additional $46.25 per month for one child under 12 to $83.25 per month for five or more children under 13.

Alberta

[11] Persons who qualify for the Assured Income for the Severely Handicapped program have higher earnings exemptions. Single persons get an exemption of $200 a month plus 25 percent of additional earnings, and families have an exemption of $775 monthly.

British Columbia

[12] On April 1, 2002, BC increased the earnings exemption for recipients under Disability Benefits Level 2 (permanently unemployable) from $200 to $300 per month.

[13] On April 1, 2002, BC eliminated all earnings exemptions for these categories of recipients.

[14] On April 1, 2002, BC eliminated all earnings exemptions for these categories of recipients.

Northwest Territories

[15] On September 1, 2001 Northwest Territories increased the earnings exemptions to $200 and $400 for singles and families respectively.

Nunavut

[16] On July 1, 2002, Nunavut increased the earnings exemption to $200 and $400 for singles and families respectively.

CONCLUSION

In 1989, all parties in the House of Commons passed a resolution to end child poverty by 2000. The deadline came and went with no improvement in the situation of poor children and their parents. Evidence about the importance of eradicating child poverty mounted, but the problem became more severe.

The federal government introduced the National Child Benefit in 1998 as its major contribution to fighting child poverty. The program is massive. By the fiscal year 2004-2005, federal government's investment in the National Child Benefit will be over $10 billion. The National Child Benefit gave all modest-income families a basic benefit to support their children. The program also had a supplement that went to the lowest income families.

This program had great potential to help reduce child poverty. Evaluations of the National Child Benefit show that it seems to have helped those families with modest incomes in which the parents have been lucky enough to find and keep work on a relatively steady basis.

Unfortunately, the deal the federal government made with the provinces and territories made a distinction between those children who are poor because their parents have regular paid jobs with low wages, and those children who are poor because their parents rely on welfare. The federal government's deal allowed the provinces and territories to take the money from the supplement out of the pockets of those parents forced to depend on welfare. The money had to be reinvested on programs for children, but the criteria for these programs are loose. Programs that are funded with the money from the clawback do not necessarily reach families on welfare.

As this report shows, parents on welfare received their child benefits from the federal government, then the province or territory took the money. The process is a little different in each jurisdiction, but in the end, it amounts to the same thing: provincial and territorial welfare officials siphoned off amounts equal to the supplement from welfare benefits. Only Newfoundland and New Brunswick refused to exercise this option from the beginning. Since then, Nova Scotia, Quebec and Manitoba reduced the amounts they claw back. In these three provinces, families on welfare still lose some of the money.

For those children unlucky enough to have parents who get their income from welfare, the results are not good. Between inflation and the clawback of the supplement to federal benefits, most welfare incomes for families lost value in the period since the National Child Benefit was introduced. In the five provinces that did not claw back – or only partially clawed back – the supplement, families on welfare were generally a little better off. In any case, welfare incomes for families remained shockingly low, in most cases below two-thirds of the poverty line. From the evidence about the impact of poverty on early child development, these are levels of destitution that are low enough to harm a child's future.

The National Council of Welfare considers the clawback of federal child benefits to be bad social policy. We agree that welfare programs should provide strong incentives to work, but we do not believe that taking any money from the poorest of the poor makes sense. As this report shows, welfare incomes are disgracefully low. There is simply no fat to cut in the budgets of people who are forced to rely on welfare.

The Council believes that a far more constructive approach to getting people off welfare would be to provide real incentives to work. The most obvious incentive for parents on welfare is the provision of high-quality affordable child care. It is overwhelmingly clear to the Council that the provision of child care is the very first step in making it possible for a parent on welfare to complete an education or training program, and then find and keep a job. It continues to astonish the Council that any social planner or politician could think otherwise.

A 2003 report on child care in Canada points out that there were regulated child care spaces for only 12.1 percent of Canadian children. In the view of the National Council of Welfare, the sooner Canada establishes a national child care system with affordable, high-quality, regulated child care, the better. Only when that system is in place will there be a realistic and reasonable incentive to work for parents on welfare.

The Council took some hope from the February 2003 federal budget. Funding for Medicare is an important part of supporting the infrastructure of Canadian social policy. The Council supports the federal budget's investment in Medicare. The Council was disappointed that the support for the medical system did not provide better support for public health. Poverty and early child development are major determinants of health. As long as we allow poverty to persist, sustaining an effective medical system will remain an elusive goal.

The Council has heard rumours that with the federal increases to the National Child Benefit that were announced in this budget, more provinces and territories will cease to claw back federal child benefits from parents on welfare. The Council recommends that the provinces and territories cease the practice of clawing back federal child benefits immediately. This would go a long way toward reducing child and family poverty in Canada and would promote better health outcomes for all.

The Council was also pleased that a national child care system finally made it to the federal budget. Study after study has made it abundantly evident that this program is essential to achieving better child health, lower child and family poverty, improved equality between women and men, and an increase in population health. This year the Standing Committee on Finance joined the voices calling for this essential program.

The Council was, however, disappointed that the federal government allotted only $25 million in the first year of the new program, and $75 million in the next year. The Council recommends in the strongest possible terms that the federal government proceed with its negotiations with the provinces and territories, and that it ensures that the architecture for a good national system is established. The Council recommends that the federal government also ensure that far higher levels of funding are allocated to the child care program as soon as negotiations are complete.

APPENDIX A: ESTIMATED NUMBER OF PEOPLE ON WELFARE BY PROVINCE AND TERRITORY

	March 31, 1995	March 31, 1996	March 31, 1997	March 31, 1998	March 31, 1999	March 31, 2000	March 31, 2001	March 31, 2002	% Change 2001-2002
NEWFOUNDLAND AND LABRADOR	71,300	72,000	71,900	64,600	59,900	59,400	54,400	52,100	-4.2%
PRINCE EDWARD ISLAND	12,400	11,700	11,100	10,900	9,800	8,400	7,900	7,500	-5.1%
NOVA SCOTIA	104,000	103,100	93,700	85,500	80,900	73,700	66,800	61,500	-7.9%
NEW BRUNSWICK	67,400	67,100	70,600	67,100	61,800	56,300	52,900	50,700	-4.2%
QUEBEC	802,200	813,200	793,300	725,700	661,300	618,900	576,600	560,800	-2.7%
ONTARIO	1,344,600	1,214,600	1,149,600	1,091,300	910,100	802,000	709,200	687,600	-3.0%
MANITOBA	85,200	85,800	79,100	72,700	68,700	63,300	60,500	60,100	-0.7%
SASKATCHEWAN	82,200	80,600	79,700	72,500	66,500	63,800	60,900	56,100	-7.9%
ALBERTA	113,200	105,600	89,800	77,000	71,900	64,800	58,000	53,800	-7.2%
BRITISH COLUMBIA	374,300	369,900	321,300	297,400	275,200	262,400	252,900	241,200	-4.6%
YUKON	2,100	1,700	2,000	2,100	1,700	1,400	1,300	1,000	-23.1%
NORTHWEST TERRITORIES	12,000	11,800	12,800	10,700	11,300	3,400	2,200	2,100	-4.5%
NUNAVUT						7,300	7,300	8,100	11.0%
CANADA	3,070,900	2,937,100	2,774,900	2,577,500	2,279,100	2,085,100	1,910,900	1,842,600	-3.6%

Source: Social Program Information and Analysis Division, Social Policy Directorate, Human Resources Development Canada

APPENDIX B: POVERTY LINE, 2002 ESTIMATE

NATIONAL COUNCIL OF WELFARE ESTIMATES OF STATISTICS CANADA'S

BEFORE-TAX LOW INCOME CUT-OFFS (1992 BASE) FOR 2002*

Family Size	Community Size				
	Cities of 500,000+	100,000-499,999	30,000-99,999	Less than 30,000	Rural Areas
1	19,256	16,516	16,401	15,261	13,307
2	24,069	20,644	20,501	19,077	16,633
3	29,934	25,676	25,497	23,725	20,687
4	36,235	31,080	30,864	28,719	25,041
5	40,505	34,743	34,501	32,103	27,993
6	44,775	38,406	38,138	35,486	30,944
7 +	49,043	42,069	41,774	38,870	33,896

Based on inflation of 2.2% from 2001 to 2002.

APPENDIX C: MAXIMUM NATIONAL CHILD BENEFIT PAYMENTS 1998-2002					
	July 1998	July 1999	July 2000	July 2001	July 2002
Canada Child Tax Benefit	$1,020	$1,020	$1,104	$1,117	$1,151
Canada Child Tax Benefit Threshold	$25,921	$25,921	$30,004	$32,000	$32,960
Additional Payment for a Child Under 7	$213	$213	$219	$221	$228
Supplement for the 1st Child in a Family	$605	$785	$977	$1,255	$1,293
Supplement for the 2nd Child in a Family	$405	$585	$771	$1,055	$1,087
National Child Benefit Supplement Threshold	$20,921	$20,921	$21,214	$21,744	$22,397

This table shows the payments by the federal government to families with children since the National Child Benefit was introduced in July 1998. The National Child Benefit consists of two payments: the basic Canada Child Tax Benefit or CCTB and the National Child Benefit Supplement or NCBS. Families with children under seven get an additional payment. Each year, the rates increased on July 1 and were in effect until June 30 of the following year.

The first row called Basic Canada Child Tax Benefit shows the annual basic benefit. The second row called Canada Child Tax Benefit Threshold shows the highest net income a family could have and still be eligible for the full Canada Child Tax Benefit. Once a family's income exceeded this amount, the federal government reduced the basic benefit. The basic federal child tax benefit is totally phased out once the net income of a family with one or two children is higher than $75,000. The third row shows the annual basic supplement paid for each child under seven.

The federal government paid a basic federal child tax benefit of $1,151 for the period beginning July 1, 2002 for each child under age 18 if the family income was under $32,960. The amounts are the same for all provinces and territories except Alberta which asked the federal government to vary these amounts. The federal government also made an additional payment of $228 for each child under age seven for the period beginning July 2002.

The fourth and fifth rows show the National Child Tax Benefit Supplement as of July 1 each year. For the first child in a family, the supplement was $1,293 on July 1, 2002 and $1,087 for the second child.

The final row called National Child Benefit Supplement Threshold shows the highest income a family could have and still get the supplement. The column for July 2002 shows that the federal government provided all families with incomes under $22,397 with the National Child Benefit Supplement.

APPENDIX D: MAXIMUM NATIONAL CHILD BENEFIT PAYMENTS FOR FAMILIES ON WELFARE 1997-2002		
January 1 to December 31	Single Parent with One Child Age 2	Couple with Two Children Ages 10 and 15
1997	$1,233	$2,040
1998	$1,535	$2,545
1999	$1,828	$3,230
2000	$2,159	$3,683
2001	$2,447	$4,250
2002	$2,633	$4,613

This table shows the National Child Benefit payments from 1997 to 2002 for a single parent with a two year old and a couple with a ten and fifteen year old. Each row includes the total payments each family received between January 1 and December 31 each year. These calculations are based on six months of payments at the previous year's rate for January to June and six months of payments at the current year's rate for July to December.

The middle column shows the total annual payment to the single-parent family. The payment includes the Canada Child Tax Benefit and the additional payment for a child under seven combined with the National Child Benefit Supplement. In the last column, the annual amounts include the Canada Child Tax Benefit and the National Child Benefit Supplement payments for a couple with a ten and fifteen year old.

MEMBERS OF THE NATIONAL COUNCIL OF WELFARE

Mr. John Murphy (Chairperson)
Canning, Nova Scotia

Ms. Doris Bernard	Radisson, Quebec
Ms. Judy Burgess	Victoria, British Columbia
Ms. Olive Crane	Mt. Stewart, Prince Edward Island
Ms. Anne Gill	Hay River, Northwest Territories
Ms. Miriam Green	Montreal, Quebec
Ms. Allyce Herle	Regina, Saskatchewan
Ms. Hope Hunter	Edmonton, Alberta
Mr. Al Kavanaugh	Riverview, New Brunswick
Mr. Greg deGroot-Maggetti	Kitchener, Ontario
Mr. David Northcott	Winnipeg, Manitoba
Ms. Marilyn Peers	Halifax, Nova Scotia
Ms. Shaunna Reid	Mount Pearl, Newfoundland
Mr. David Welch	Ottawa, Ontario

****

Director: Joanne Roulston

Senior Researcher: Olufunmilola (Lola) Fabowalé

Researcher: Julie Stevenson

Administration and Information Officer: Louise Gunville

Administrative Assistant: Claudette Mann

NATIONAL COUNCIL OF WELFARE

The National Council of Welfare was established by the Government Organization Act, 1969, as a citizens' advisory body to the federal government. It advises the Minister of Human Resources Development on matters of concern to low-income Canadians.

The Council consists of members drawn from across Canada and appointed by the Governor-in-Council. All are private citizens and serve in their personal capacities rather than as representatives of organizations or agencies. The membership of the Council has included welfare recipients, public housing tenants and other low-income people, as well as educators, social workers and people involved in voluntary or charitable organizations.

Reports by the National Council of Welfare deal with a wide range of issues on poverty and social policy in Canada, including income security programs, welfare reform, medicare, poverty lines and poverty statistics, the retirement income system, taxation, labour market issues, social services and legal aid.

On peut se procurer des exemplaires en français de toutes les publications du Conseil national du bien-être social, en s'adressant au Conseil national du bien-être social, 9e étage, 112, rue Kent, Ottawa, Ontario, K1A 0J9, sous notre site web au www.ncwcnbes.net ou sous forme de courrier électronique au ncw@magi.com.